metalworking

First Edition

Lithographed in U.S.A.

DR. WILBUR R. MILLER
University of Missouri — Columbia
Columbia, Missouri

DR. VICTOR E. REPP
Bowling Green State University
Bowling Green, Ohio

DR. MARION E. MADDOX
University of Arkansas
Fayetteville, Arkansas

WILLARD J. McCARTHY
Illinois State University
Normal, Illinois

LAVON B. SMITH
Fayetteville, Arkansas

OSWALD A. LUDWIG
Henry Ford High School
Detroit, Michigan

basic industrial arts

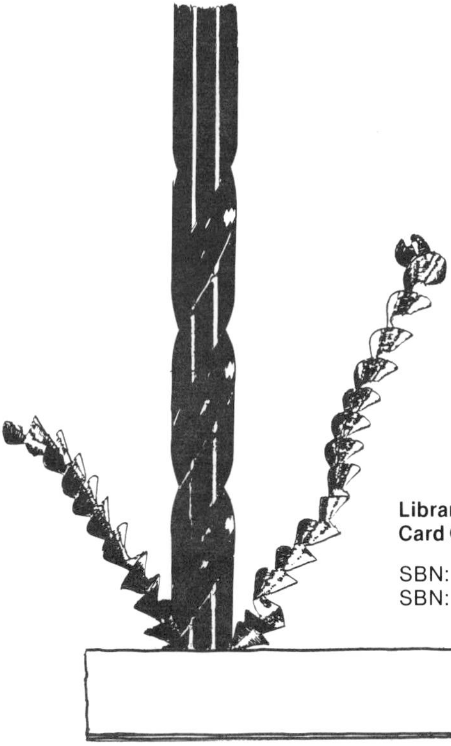

Library of Congress
Card Catalog Number: **78-53387**

SBN: 87345-784-6 Paperback
SBN: 87345-792-7 Hardbound

Copyright © 1978

McKNIGHT

**Publishing Company
Bloomington, Illinois**

TABLE OF CONTENTS

Chapter 5   FORGING AND FORMING MW-51

Chapter 6   SHEET METALWORK MW-59

Chapter 7   ART METALWORK MW-70

Chapter 8   CASTING MW-80

791181

INTRODUCTION TO
METALS AND METALWORKING

Chapter **1**

THE IMPORTANCE OF METALS

Metals are used everywhere. They are widely used to construct transportation vehicles. Aircraft and spacecraft, automobiles, buses and trucks, railroad cars, bicycles and motorcycles, and ships and submarines are made of metals. Steel and other structural metals are used to build roads, bridges, tunnels, and buildings. See Fig. 1-1. Home appliances are also made of metals. They include stoves, washing machines, clothes dryers, toasters, refrigerators, furnaces, and air conditioners.

A large part of the labor force is employed in metalworking careers. These workers have different levels of education and skills. Some are semiskilled workers and craftsmen (a level of skill identified by trade unions). Others are technicians, technologists, and engineers who specialize in different fields of metalwork.

Bethlehem Steel

Fig. 1-1.   Metals are used everywhere.

THE NATURE OF METALS

Metals used in industry are classed in two general groups, **ferrous** and **nonferrous**. The **ferrous metals** are those made from the element (Fe) or iron. The many types of steel as well as pig iron, cast iron, and wrought iron are classed as ferrous metals. **Non-ferrous metals** are those produced from metallic elements other than iron. The most common of these are aluminum, copper, tin, zinc, lead, nickel, gold, silver, and platinum.

Two or more metals are often combined to form an **alloy.** An alloy has different characteristics than each of the metals. Steel is often combined with chromium, manganese, or nickel to form **steel alloys.** Aluminum may be combined with other metals to form **aluminum alloys.** Sometimes the names of the metals being combined are not used when the metals are alloyed. For example copper and zinc are combined to form brass, or copper and tin are combined to form bronze.

RAW MATERIALS

A metallic ore is the natural resource from which a metal is produced. Iron is produced from **iron ore.** Copper is produced from **copper ore.** Aluminum is produced from an ore called **bauxite.**

Ore is found in deposits beneath the surface of the earth. There are deposits in many different places around the earth. When a rich deposit is found, it is mined by one of several methods.

U.S. Steel

Fig. 1-2.   An open-pit mine provides for both truck and rail transportation.

U.S. Steel

Fig. 1-3.   Stockpile of iron ore, coke, and limestone.

The traditional method of mining uses a **deep shaft.** Tunnels are dug from the shaft into the deposit. The ore is carried to the shaft and raised to the surface. It is then transported to a processing location.

A shallow deposit that runs parallel to the earth's surface may be **strip mined.** Parallel trenches are dug from one edge of the deposit to the other. The ore is removed. Unwanted dirt and foreign material are placed in trenches dug earlier. This process can leave the land rather rough unless care is taken to smooth the piles before the mining operation leaves the area. Coal is commonly mined in this way.

The most thorough type of mining is the **open-pit mine,** Fig. 1-2. This method is similar to strip mining with several exceptions. All of the materials, including the waste, is removed from the mine.

PRODUCTION OF IRON

Iron ore is stockpiled near the blast furnaces at the mill. There are also stockpiles of coke (similar to charcoal) and limestone, Fig. 1-3. These are the materials needed to produce iron.

The blast furnace is a steel cylinder several stories high, Fig. 1-4. It is lined with firebrick to withstand high temperatures. There are several other vertical steel cylinders near the blast furnace. These are used to heat the air that is blasted into the furnace.

The blast furnace **separates the iron from the iron ore** in a continuous operation. It runs day and night. It is shut down only for repairs or maintenance. Iron ore, limestone, and coke are dumped into the top of the blast furnace. Each layer of these materials is put on the top of layers already placed in the furnace. When the layer is first placed into the blast furnace it is cool. See view **A** of Fig. 1-5. The layer will move down into the blast furnace, as shown in view **B.** Hot gases passing up through the furnace and coke burning in all the layers cause the top layer to get hotter. The layer has a temperature of about 3000° F (1649° C) as it nears the bottom of the furnace. See view **C** of Fig. 1-5. The blast of hot air has caused the temperature to rise above the melting point of the iron in the ore. The iron will now melt. **It will separate** from the other materials of the ore. The heavy molten iron flows to the bottom of the furnace. See view **D.**

The burned coke and the limestone combine and form a layer on the top of the molten iron. This layer is called slag. Slag is a waste product of iron production. It is poured off into a slag ladle. The molten iron is then poured out of the blast furnace into a ladle. It is poured into molds called **pigs.** When it cools, it is called **pig iron.**

The pigs are melted and poured into a shaped mold to make cast iron. Cast iron is brittle but hard.

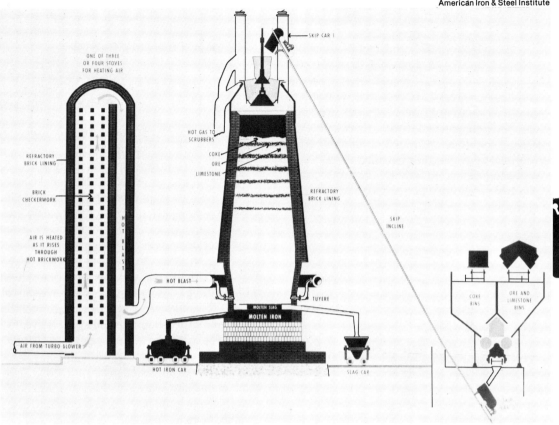

Fig. 1-4.   Blast furnace.

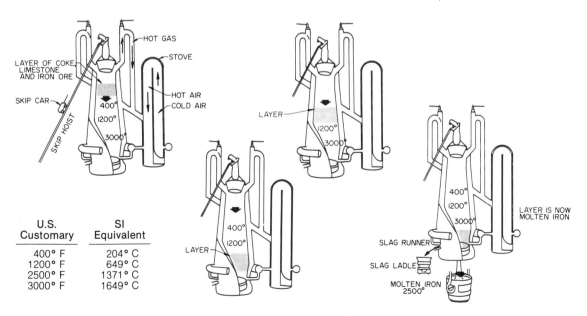

U.S. Customary	SI Equivalent
400° F	204° C
1200° F	649° C
2500° F	1371° C
3000° F	1649° C

Fig. 1-5.   Layer of coke, limestone, and iron ore as it moves through the furnace.

Pig iron has a carbon content of about 3% to 5%. Carbon can be removed by burning it out of the iron in a special furnace. When all of the carbon is removed, a material known as **wrought iron** is produced. Wrought iron has quite different characteristics than cast iron. Wrought iron is **not brittle.** It is tough and can be formed by bending and twisting.

Cast iron has a carbon content of about 1.7% to 6%. Wrought iron has a carbon content of less than .04%. Different amounts of carbon left in the iron produce iron with different properties.

PRODUCTION OF STEEL

Steel is made from pig iron. The process is similar to that used for making different kinds of cast iron. Steel has a carbon content from .05% to 1.5%. It can be made by either removing carbon from pig iron or adding carbon to wrought iron. Steel having the primary contents of carbon and iron is called **carbon steel.**

Several processes are used to make steel. One is the **Bessemer process.** It is named after the man who developed the process. The main piece of equipment used in the process is the Bessemer converter. It is a large pear-shaped tank with an open top. See Fig. 1-6. Molten pig iron is poured into the converter. Air jets force air up through the tank. The oxygen in the air causes the carbon to be burned out of the iron. The tank is then tipped to pour the iron into a ladle. The steel is then poured into **ingots** (molds) to harden.

Oxygen is now used more often than air for the steelmaking process. When this practice is followed, the process is known as the **basic-oxygen process.**

Three other methods of making steel are named after the types of furnaces used to melt the iron. The **open hearth furnace** has large doors in the front, Fig. 1-7. The material to be melted is placed on the hearth through an open

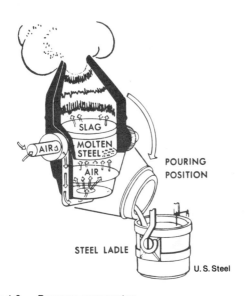

Fig. 1-6.   Bessemer converter.

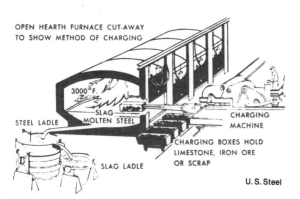

Fig. 1-7.   Open-hearth furnace.

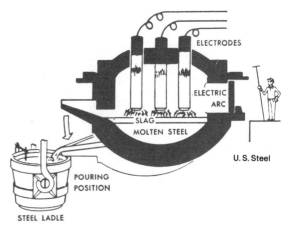

Fig. 1-8.   Electric furnace.

door. A flame of burning gas or oxygen and air is directed at the iron, causing it to melt. Large amounts of steel can be made this way.

An **electric furnace** is used in processing high-grade steels. The heat comes from an electric arc between the metal being heated and carbon electrodes above the metal. See Fig. 1-8. The electric furnace can produce temperatures even higher than with the other methods.

The earliest process for steelmaking used the **crucible furnace.** A crucible is a small container about 18″ (457 mm) high and 12″ (305 mm) in diameter. The crucible is made from graphite or other material that can withstand the high temperatures. Wrought iron is melted and carbon is added to produce crucible steel.

The steel that is produced by all of these methods can be poured into ingots. Or the steel can be directly processed into sheets, rods, beams, or any other form.

PRODUCTION OF ALUMINUM

Aluminum is not found in metallic form in nature. Bauxite or aluminum ore contains aluminum chemically combined with other elements. Merely removing dirt, rocks, and other minerals in the ore does not leave metallic aluminum. The production of aluminum is much more difficult and costly than the production of iron and steel.

Bauxite must pass through a long process in order to produce aluminum. Note the steps in this process, Fig. 1-9. First, the bauxite goes through a process that produces alumina or aluminum oxide. The alumina is then changed into metallic aluminum by a reduction process called **electrolysis.**

PROPERTIES OF METAL

Metal has chemical, electrical, and physical properties. These properties help to determine the type of metal that should be used for a specific job.

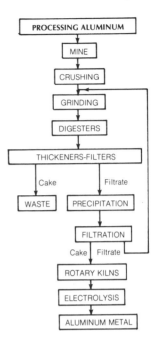

Fig. 1-9.   Processing aluminum.

Aluminum Company of America

Fig. 1-10.   Can the metal be welded?

Chemical Properties

1. Oxidation, or the effect of oxygen.
2. Melting point.
3. The effect of acids and other chemical substances.
4. Ability to weld. Can the metal be fused by heat? See Fig. 1-10.
5. Ability to harden. To what extent can the hardness be changed by heat treatment?

Electrical Properties

1. Ability to conduct electricity.
2. Ability to give off light and heat with electric current flow.

Physical Properties

1. Brittleness. The extent to which metal will crack or break when dropped or subjected to impact.
2. Ductility. The ease with which it can be drawn or stretched into wire.
3. Elasticity. The ability to return to its original shape after bending or twisting.
4. Hardness. The ability to resist denting and scratching.
5. Machinability. The ease with which it can be cut, ground, and polished, Fig. 1-11.
6. Malleability. The ability to be formed by hammering and bending.

Metals have different properties. An engineer or product designer selects the materials to be used in a product on the basis of their properties. The six common properties of metals are density, resistance to corrosion, hardness, toughness, brittleness, and tensile strength.

Density refers to the weight of the metal. The density may be indicated in pounds per cubic inch (lb./in.^{3}) or pounds per cubic foot (kilograms per cubic meter). The density of steel is 0.284 lb./in.^{3} (7861 kg/m^3). Aluminum,

which is much lighter in weight, has a density of 0.097 lb./in.^{3} (2685 kg/m^3). Hence, steel is nearly three times as dense or as heavy as the same volume of aluminum.

Corrosion resistance is the ability of a metal to resist chemical action, such as rusting. Aluminum, stainless steel, and copper resist corrosion much better than steel.

Hardness means resistance to penetration. Steel is much harder than lead or pure aluminum. Some steels can be made even harder by heat treatment processes. They can be made so hard that they will cut other metals.

Toughness in metal refers to its ability to withstand shock or heavy impact without breaking. A metal that ranks high in toughness will generally bend or deform before it breaks. When steel is hardened by heat treatment, it loses some of its toughness. Files or drills, which are hardened by heat treatment, will usually break before they bend.

Brittleness refers to the ease with which metals will break without bending or deforming greatly. Glass is very brittle. Hardened tool steels and gray cast iron are quite brittle when compared to ordinary unhardened steels.

Tensile strength means resistance to being pulled apart. It is the force needed to pull apart a piece of metal which has one square inch (6.45 sq. centimeters) of cross-sectional area. Tensile strength is expressed in terms of thousands of pounds per square inch (meganewtons per square meter). For example, pure soft aluminum has a tensile strength of about 13,000 psi (89 632 meganewtons). Soft low-carbon steel has a tensile strength of about 69,000 psi (475 738 meganewtons). The tensile strength of certain kinds of tool steels can be increased to about 200,000 psi (1 369 951 meganewtons) by heat-treatment processes.

SAFETY IN DRESSING FOR METALWORK

Be Clean and Neat

A worker who is clean and neat is usually a safe worker and most often does clean, neat

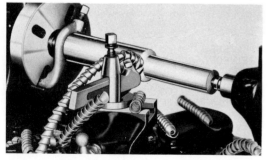

South Bend Lathe, Inc.

Fig. 1-11. Can the metal be cut, ground, and polished?

SHORT HAIR OR WEAR A SMALL CAP

SAFETY GLASSES WITH SIDE SHIELDS

NO SWEATER

SCARF OR TIE TUCKED BETWEEN THE 1ST AND 2ND BUTTONS

SLEEVES ROLLED UP OR CUT OFF ABOVE THE ELBOWS

NO TORN POCKETS

CLEAN APRON THAT FITS CLOSELY AROUND THE BODY

NO WRIST WATCH, RING OR GLOVES

APRON HANGS DOWN TO THE KNEES

STRONG APRON STRINGS TIED AT THE BACK

Fig. 1-12.   Dressed safely for work.

work. Never wear loose or torn clothing. It may be caught by a moving part of the machine and pull the worker into gears or blades.

Apron

Wear a clean apron made of heavy canvas. It should hang down to the knees as shown in Fig. 1-12. Apron strings should be strong and long enough so that they can be tied properly at the back. Strings tied in front may be caught in a machine. The apron should fit snugly on the chest and around the waist. Apron strings that cross on the back fit best. They pull the apron up close to the chest and snugly around the body. Pockets should be sewed on properly. A torn pocket may get caught in a machine.

Aprons should be washed regularly. An apron is for keeping clothing clean, not for wiping dirty hands. It is best to own two aprons. One may be worn while the other is washed.

Necktie

The long or flowing necktie should be removed entirely. Or it can be tucked into the shirt between the first and second buttons as

shown in Fig. 1-12. This will keep the necktie from getting tangled in a machine.

Gloves

Never wear gloves around a machine because they may get caught. However, workers must wear gloves when welding.

Sleeves

It is safer to wear short sleeves than long sleeves. Long sleeves should either fit the arm closely or be rolled up above the elbow. Loose or torn sleeves, or sleeves that are not rolled up may get caught in a machine.

Wristwatches and Rings

Wristwatches and rings are a definite hazard to safety. They should be removed while a person works around machinery or works with electricity.

Shoes

Open-toed sandals, canvas shoes, and other soft shoes do not protect your feet. Leather dress shoes and work shoes give much better protection. They should be worn while working in shops and laboratories. Industrial quality safety shoes give even greater protection against crushing type accidents. See Fig. 1-13.

STEEL REINFORCEMENT

Fig. 1-13. Safety shoe with steel reinforced toe.

Eye Protection

Many states require teachers and students to wear safety glasses while working in school shops and laboratories. Visitors should also be protected. Wear safety glasses with side shields, goggles, and face shields. They should meet or exceed state and federal rules for safety. **Protect your eyes.** Be sure you learn and observe the eye protection rules at your school.

SAFETY IN WORKING WITH METALS

Learn to use machines, equipment, tools, and materials correctly. You must follow safety rules and safety practices in order to avoid accidents and personal injury. The following rules, precautions, and procedures should be observed:

1. **Always** tell the teacher right away when you are injured in the shop or laboratory, no matter how slight the injury.
2. **Always** have proper first aid applied to minor injuries. **Always** see a doctor for proper attention to bad cuts, bruises, burns, or other injuries.
3. Wear glasses, goggles, or a face shield of an approved type at all times in the shop or laboratory.
4. Oil or grease on the floor is hazardous and can cause slipping. Always clean up oil or grease right away.
5. Place oily rags or other flammable wiping materials in the proper containers.
6. Keep aisles and pathways clear of excess stock, remnants, or waste. Store long metal bars in the proper area.
7. Return all tools or machine accessories to the proper storage areas after use.
8. Operate machines or equipment only when your teacher tells you to do so.
9. Avoid shouting, whistling, or horseplay when in the shop.
10. Never touch metal that you think is hot. If in doubt, touch the metal with the moistened tip of your finger to determine whether it is hot.
11. When you approach people who are operating a machine, wait until they have finished that part of an operation or process before you talk to them.
12. Do not touch any moving part of machinery.
13. Do not lean on a machine that someone else is operating.
14. Do not operate a machine until the cutting tools and the workpiece are mounted securely.
15. Be sure that all of the safety devices with which a machine is equipped are in the proper place and order before you use the machine.
16. If more than one person is to work on a certain machine, only one person should operate the controls or switches.
17. Never leave a machine while it is running or in motion.
18. Always stop a machine before oiling, cleaning, or making adjustments on it.
19. Always use a brush or a stick of wood to remove metal chips from a machine that has been turned off. Otherwise, you may be cut by sharp chips.
20. Do not use your hands to try to stop a machine, such as a drill press spindle or a lathe spindle.
21. Do not touch moving belts or pulleys.
22. Always be sure that the machine has stopped before changing a V-belt.
23. Before starting a machine, be sure to remove excess tools, oil, or waste.
24. Ask for help from a fellow worker when a heavy machine accessory or other heavy objects must be moved. Always **lift with your legs,** not your back.
25. Do not work in restricted areas which are marked off as safety zones.
26. Be sure that everyone around you is wearing approved safety glasses, goggles, or a safety shield if your teacher allows you to blow metal chips from a machine with compressed air.

27. Know the location of the nearest fire alarm in the building in case of fire. Also, learn where the nearest fire extinguisher is and ask you teacher to explain how it is operated.
28. Always place flammable materials, such as paint thinners, lacquers, and solvents, in a metal cabinet away from open flames.

SAFETY IN USING HAND TOOLS

Personal injury often results from using hand tools, Fig. 1-14. Follow these safety rules or safe work practices when you use hand tools:

1. Use the right tool for the job to be done.
2. See that tools and your hands are clean and free of grease or oil before use.
3. Use sharp cutting tools. Dull tools cause accidents because you would apply more force to use them.
4. Carry sharp-edge tools with their points and cutting edges pointing downward.
5. Do not let the heads of cold chisels and punches mushroom or crack. They should be properly dressed or repaired.

Fig. 1-14. Many accidents happen when hand tools are used.

6. When using a chisel, always chip in a direction that will prevent flying chips from striking others.
7. Choose the correct type of wrench for the job and use it properly. You can injure your knuckles or hand if the wrench slips. See Fig. 1-15.
8. When using a file, be sure that it has a snug-fitting handle. Otherwise, you could hurt your hand on the sharp tang of the file.
9. When you pass tools to others, give them the handle first.
10. Always report damaged tools to the teacher. Damaged tools can cause injuries.
11. Tools should always be wiped free of grease or dirt after use. Return them to the proper storage location.

CAREER OPPORTUNITIES

Your home, pleasures, and way of life will depend greatly on the income and satisfaction your job provides. Before you make a career choice, know everything you can about the occupation which you plan to make your career.

Meaning of Skill and Knowledge

Skill results from the training of your body to do certain things. Knowledge comes from learning. To learn a trade or to become a technician, you must acquire both skills and knowledge. To work in a skilled trade, you must be able to apply knowledge. To learn a trade or to become a technician or an engineer, you must know something about mathematics, drawing, science, and other subjects. You must know why things are done in a certain way. You also need to know much of the information in this book. It will help you communicate with and understand the people who work in the many metalworking industries.

OCCUPATIONS IN METALWORKING

Jobs in metalworking are classed according to the knowledge, skill, and length of train-

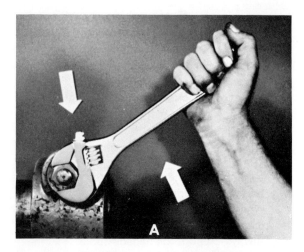

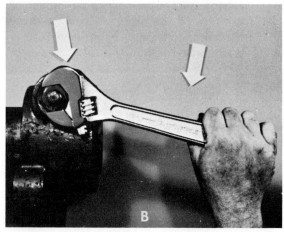

Fig. 1-15. Use a wrench properly.
- A. Wrong. Do not push on the handle.
- B. Right. Pull on the handle.
- C. Use an offset box wrench when possible.

ing needed to do the required work. Here are some common types of workers needed.
1. Unskilled workers
2. Semiskilled workers
3. Skilled workers
4. Technicians
5. Technologists
6. Engineers

Unskilled Workers

Unskilled workers need little or no special training to do their work. As an example, laborers who handle and move materials by hand are in this group. The percentage of unskilled workers in the total labor force is decreasing. It will probably continue to decrease in the years ahead.

Semiskilled Workers

Semiskilled workers must have some special training for the work they do. Their training period may range from several days to about one year. They may get training in a school shop. Sometimes their employer provides training on the job.

Examples of metalworking jobs in the semiskilled group include assembly-line workers in factories, inspectors, maintenance mechanics, painters, spot welders, and punch press operators. Machine tool operators are also thought of as semiskilled workers. They may be drill press operators, lathe operators, milling machine operators, or planer and shaper operators. There are operators of nearly every kind of special production machine tool.

Experience can be gained in class in high school, vocational school, or machine shop. It will be helpful in getting work and advancing more rapidly as a machine tool operator. It is also valuable in getting a job in many kinds of semiskilled jobs in the metalworking industry.

Skilled Workers

A skilled trade is often learned by combining shop instruction, classroom instruction, and training on the job. Most often, classroom instruction includes mathematics, blueprint reading, technical theory, and science. Skilled trades in metalworking include many kinds of jobs. Some of them are machinist, layout artist, tool-and-die maker, instrument maker, boiler-maker, welder, sheet metalworker, molder, and heat treater.

Apprenticeship Method

An apprentice is employed to learn a trade. Skills may be learned from a master of the trade or under the direction of a company. The apprenticeship training period may vary from two to six years. The apprenticeship period for becoming a machinist or tool-and-die maker, for example, is usually four or five years. When the apprenticeship is completed, the worker becomes a **journeyman.** This is a level of skill identified by trade unions. A journeyman has met the minimum skills needed to enter a trade. A document is issued to show that apprenticeship training has been completed. It specifies the trade or occupation in which the worker is qualified. Many employers and labor unions accept this document as a worker's entry into the trade.

Engineers

Engineers plan, design, and direct construction. Their work may be in the building of roads, bridges, tunnels, factories, office buildings, waterworks, dams, or mines. Or they may be involved with automobiles, aircraft and spacecraft, ships, railroads, power plants, electrical appliances, electronic equipment, machinery, and engines. Some engineers plan, design and direct the construction of radio and television stations. Engineers must have college degrees. They must like mathematics and drawing, and must know a lot about physics and chemistry.

Technicians

Technical jobs are among the fastest growing groups of occupations in the United States, Fig. 1-16. Technicians must know how to apply

theories of science and mathematics. They help translate scientific ideas into useful products or services. Sometimes they work indirectly with scientists, engineers, or industrial managers. It has been said that industry needs several technicians for every professional engineer.

In general, the job of technician requires high school graduation and two years of technical training. This training is available in various types of schools. This includes technical institutes, junior colleges, community colleges, area vocational or technical schools, armed forces schools, technical-vocational high schools, private technical schools, and extension divisions of colleges and universities.

Aircraft and Engine Mechanics

Aircraft and engine mechanics repair, inspect, and overhaul airplanes. They may do emergency repairs or major repairs. They may make frequent inspections. The mechanic should be able to measure with micrometers, use hand tools, and run such machine tools as the drill press and the grinder. The work is greasy and dirty. Some work has to be done outdoors. Aircraft and engine mechanics should have a high school education and should attend a technical school or institute.

The Foxboro Company

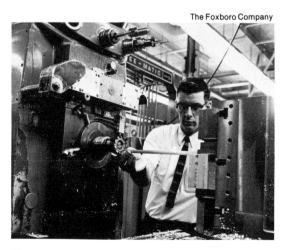

Fig. 1-16. A technician checks final program of a numerically controlled machine tool.

Auto Mechanics

An auto mechanic services and repairs mechanical, electrical, and body parts. This would involve cars, buses, trucks, and other gasoline-powered vehicles. The mechanic should be able to measure with micrometers, use many hand tools, and run the drill press and the grinder. The work is greasy and dirty. Some work may be done outdoors.

An auto mechanic should have at least a high school education. A person who has done metalwork can learn more quickly.

The auto mechanic must guard against gasoline fumes and explosions. The mechanic must also avoid the danger of inhaling the poisonous carbon monoxide gas.

Bench Mechanics

Bench mechanics work at a bench with hand tools. They must read blueprints. Mostly, they repair parts that have been disassembled from a machine or vehicle. This includes carburetors, transmission, and engines.

Drill Press Operators

Drill press operators earn a living by running a drill press, Fig. 1-17. They can do many different operations on the drill press, set up the work, and sometimes sharpen drills. A worker can learn to run a drill press in a week or, at most, in a few months.

Diemakers

The diemaker makes metal forms or patterns, called **dies**. These are used in punch presses to stamp out forms in metal. Automobile fenders are made with such dies. These dies must be exact, or the many hundreds or thousands of pieces made with them will be wrong. Diemakers can set up and run any machine and use any tool in the shop. They must read blueprints, make sketches, use layout tools, and measure with micrometers. See Fig. 1-18.

Coremakers

A coremaker makes cores used to form holes or hollow parts in castings. This makes the castings lighter so that less metal will have to be cut away afterwards. The coremaker should know mathematics and how to read blueprints. A worker may learn the trade in a foundry during an apprenticeship of about four years.

The Clausing Corp.

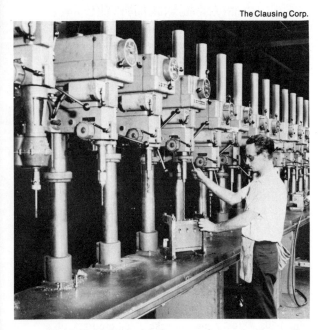

Fig. 1-17. A bank of drill presses for production work.

Fig. 1-18. A diemaker measures the size of a die.

Forge Operators

A forge operator, also called a hammer operator, runs a drop hammer on which automobile axles, wrenches, and other things are forged. The forge operator must know about iron and steel and how to read blueprints. The worker needs at least a high school education and must be strong and healthy. The work is hot, heavy, dirty and noisy. The danger of being burned by hot metal is ever present.

Heat Treaters

A heat treater does heat-treatment operations on steel and other metals. This worker must know how to harden, temper, case harden, anneal, and normalize metal. The work is often learned by working in the heat-treating department of a factory. A heat treater should have at least a high school education. The work is hot. There is danger of being burned by hot metal and hot liquids. The heat treater must sometimes guard against poisonous fumes.

Inspectors

An inspector checks materials, parts or articles while they are being made or right after they are finished. Inspectors must read blueprints. They must know the different kinds of fits and the use of all kinds of measuring tools. Inspectors should have at least a high school or trade school education.

Jewelers

The jeweler makes high-grade jewelry of platinum, gold, and silver. The quality of this work requires good eyesight. Most of it is done while the jeweler looks through an eye loupe or magnifying glass. The jeweler must know how to run a jeweler's lathe and other small hand and machine tools. Jewelers should have a high school or trade school education. They should learn the trade as an apprentice.

Lathe Operators

A lathe operator uses the lathe, Fig. 1-19. The operator can do different operations on it, set up the work, and sharpen the needed tools.

A worker can learn to run a lathe in three months to a year. A high school or trade school education is needed for this job.

Machine Setup Workers

The machine setup workers specialize in getting machine tools ready for operation. They keep them adjusted. See Fig. 1-20. Machine setup workers may be fully qualified machinists. Some learned how to set these machines by observing this while working as a machine operator. They must know how to read blueprints and to use all kinds of measuring tools and gages.

Rex Chainbelt Inc.

Fig. 1-19.   Operating a turret lathe.

Fig. 1-20.   A machine operator makes an adjustment to the machine.

PLANNING AND DRAWING

Chapter **2**

MAKING A PRODUCT PLAN

Before you can build a product of your own design, you should prepare a product plan. A product plan has all the information needed for successful construction. A good plan includes:

1. A working drawing of the product. This could be a carefully sketched freehand drawing, a pictorial drawing, or a sketch.
2. A bill of materials.
3. A list of steps, in proper order, for making the product. See the planning sheet in Fig. 2-1.
4. Approval of your teacher before making the product.

As you plan for a product, you will use procedures like those used in industry. Every item made, whether it is a tin can or an automobile, must be carefully planned before it is produced. Working drawings must be made for each part of the product. The proper materials must be selected for each part. Costs must be determined. Tools, equipment and machinery must be provided. Then the steps in manufacturing must be planned to produce the product at the least cost. Your plan will include much of the kind of work done by manufacturing engineers, industrial technologists, technicians, and skilled workers.

MAKING A BILL OF MATERIALS

You must have the correct metal before you can make a metal product. Therefore, you will need to know how to specify and order metals. The working drawing gives all of the information you need to make a bill of materials.

This bill of materials should be made in the form shown in Fig. 2-1.

A bill of materials should show:
1. Parts of the product. They should be identified by numbers or letters.
2. Number of pieces needed for each part.
3. Size of the material.
4. Shape and kind of material.
5. Standard parts used in the product.
6. Unit cost of the material. This would be cost per pound, per foot, per square foot, etc. Or, it might be cost per kilogram, per meter, per square meter, etc.
7. Total cost of the materials.

STANDARD PARTS

A standard part is one that is made by several companies and is the same part, no matter who makes it. Hardware, such as bolts, nuts, rivets, screws, and washers are made to standard sizes and shapes. They are called standard parts. Catalogs give information about standard parts and materials.

STANDARD STOCK

Standard stock refers to materials that are used in the making of finished products. They have certain sizes and shapes. Steel as it comes from the steel mill is also standard stock. Standard stock is bought from metal wholesalers. These wholesalers keep a supply of each shape in many sizes. Common shapes of stock are shown in Fig. 2-2.

Product Planning Sheet

Name _____ Grade _____
Product _____ Hour _____
Source of product idea, if other than your own design _____
_____
Estimated Time_____ Actual Time_____ Approved_____

BILL OF MATERIALS

| Part No. | No. of Pieces | Size | | | Material | Unit Cost | Total Cost |
		T	W	L			

Total Cost _____

Manufacturing Procedure
1. Select standard stock.
2. Mark stock to length or overall size.
3. Cut standard stock.
4. Make part **A.**
    a.
    b.
    c.
    d. etc.

5. Make part **B.**
    a.
    b.
    c.
    d. etc.
6. Assemble the product.
    a.
    b. etc.
7. Inspect.
8. Apply finish.
9. Inspect.

Fig. 2-1.   A form like this planning sheet may be used to plan your product.

Measuring Standard Stock

The size given on the bill of materials is the size of the standard stock that you will order. The size given on the working drawing is the finished size. This size, for any part, must have added to it the extra metal that is needed to finish the object to size. Standard stock is described as follows:

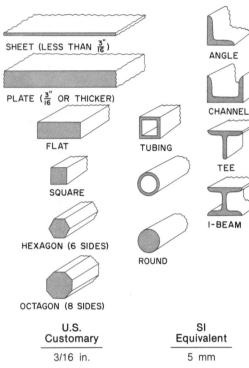

SHEET (LESS THAN $\frac{3''}{16}$)

PLATE ($\frac{3''}{16}$ OR THICKER)

FLAT

TUBING

SQUARE

HEXAGON (6 SIDES)

ROUND

OCTAGON (8 SIDES)

ANGLE

CHANNEL

TEE

I-BEAM

U.S. Customary	SI Equivalent
3/16 in.	5 mm

Fig. 2-2.   Shapes of standard metal stock.

Flat Sheet or Strip
Thickness × width × length, for example:
1/8″ × 1 3/4″ × 4 1/4″
(3 mm × 45 mm × 108 mm)
Square Bar
Thickness × width × length, for example:
1″ × 1″ × 4 1/4″
(25 mm × 25 mm × 108 mm)
Round Bar
Diameter × length, for example:
2″ dia. × 4 1/4″
(51 mm dia. × 108 mm)
Hexagonal and Octagonal Bar
Distance across flat sides × length, for example:
1 1/4″ × 4 1/4″
(32 mm × 108 mm)

Tubing
Outside dimensions × wall thickness × length, as:
7/8″ dia. × .049 wall × 12″ and 1″ × 1″ × .062 wall × 18″
(22 mm dia. × 1.245 mm wall × 305 mm and 25 mm × 25 mm × 1.575 mm wall × 457 mm)
Structural Shapes
Overall cross-sectional dimensions × shape × wall thickness × length, for example:
1 1/2″ × 1 1/2″ angle × 3/16″ wall × 36″
(38 mm × 38 mm angle × 4.76 mm wall × 914 mm)

Suppose you want to know the length of metal needed to make a scroll or spiral. You can make the shape out of soft wire and then straighten it out and measure the length.

WORKING DRAWINGS

A working drawing gives all the information workers need to make a product or object. It is a drawing from which the workers work, as shown in Fig. 2-5. It allows workers to make objects exactly alike, even in different factories. This makes the parts interchangeable. Automobile parts are made in different parts of the country. Yet, when assembled, they fit perfectly. The working drawing makes this possible. It must show the following items:
1. Shape of every part of the object.
2. Sizes of all parts.
3. Kind of material.
4. Kind of finish.
5. How many pieces of each part are wanted.

A **mechanical drawing** is a working drawing that is made with drawing instruments. It is made by the drafter or technical artist in the drafting room. Drafting includes both mechanical drawing and sketching.

Views

Each view of a working drawing shows the outline or shape of the object as seen from that side. To show all of an object, two or more

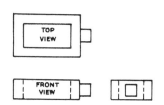

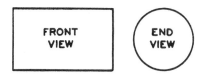

Fig. 2-3.   Front and top views of a cylinder.

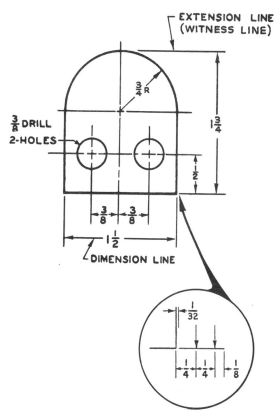

Fig. 2-4.   Front and end views of a cylinder.

views are needed. Some objects can be described with only one view. The drafter draws only those views needed. A working drawing of a cylinder needs only two views, the front view and top view, Fig. 2-3. The drawing may show the front view and end view when the cylinder lies on its side. Some objects need three views: front, top, and end (or side) views. It will help you to draw these views if you can imagine that the object is in a glass box, Fig. 2-4. The views are drawn on the front, top, and end of the imaginary box. When the box is unfolded, the views will be in their correct positions.

Dimensions are most often read from the bottom or right side of the drawing sheet. Some drafters make all dimensions read from the bottom of the sheet. See Fig. 2-5. Fractions must be made with a horizontal line, as $\frac{1}{2}, \frac{3}{4}$ When all dimensions are in inches, the inch marks (") can be omitted. If they are all in millimeters, the symbol (mm) can be omitted.

The distance from one hole to another is measured as the distance from the center of the one hole to the center of the other. Dimensions

U.S. Customary	SI Equivalent
1/16 in.	1.6 mm
1/8 in.	3.2 mm
3/8 in.	9.5 mm
1/2 in.	12.7 mm
3/4 in.	19.1 mm
1-1/4 in.	31.7 mm
1-5/16 in.	33.0 mm
1-1/2 in.	38.0 mm
1-3/4 in.	44.0 mm
2-1/2 in.	63.5 mm

Fig. 2-5.   A working drawing shows centerlines and dimensions.

between holes should always be given from center to center. The worker in the shop measures that way. See Fig. 2-5. Measurements are always made from the center of a circle or arc.

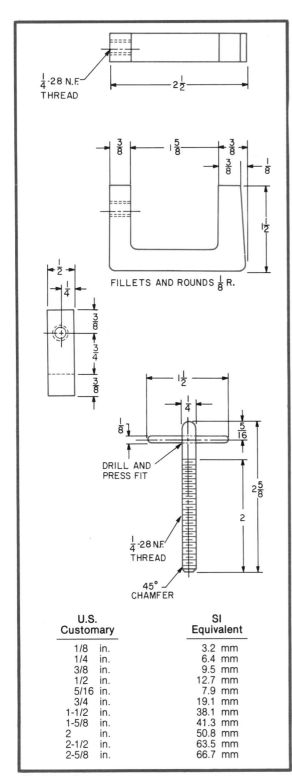

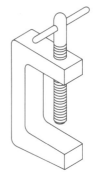

Fig. 2-7. An assembly drawing showing how the parts of the C-clamp fit together.

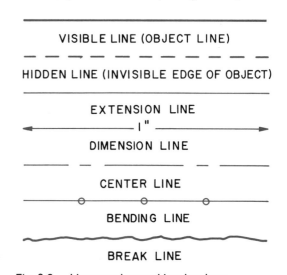

VISIBLE LINE (OBJECT LINE)

HIDDEN LINE (INVISIBLE EDGE OF OBJECT)

EXTENSION LINE

DIMENSION LINE

CENTER LINE

BENDING LINE

BREAK LINE

Fig. 2-8. Lines used on working drawings.

U.S. Customary	SI Equivalent
1/8 in.	3.2 mm
1/4 in.	6.4 mm
3/8 in.	9.5 mm
1/2 in.	12.7 mm
5/16 in.	7.9 mm
3/4 in.	19.1 mm
1-1/2 in.	38.1 mm
1-5/8 in.	41.3 mm
2 in.	50.8 mm
2-1/2 in.	63.5 mm
2-5/8 in.	66.7 mm

Fig. 2-6. Detail drawings of the parts of a C-clamp.

READING WORKING DRAWINGS

A working drawing uses the language of all mechanical occupations. This includes the drafting room, shop, and manufacturing plant. In fact, all industry uses it. A working drawing shows all the parts and their dimensions, Fig. 2-6. An assembly drawing shows how all of the parts fit together, Fig. 2-7.

To read a working drawing, you must know what certain kinds of lines, signs, and abbreviations mean. To become a mechanic, you must first learn to read this language.

Lines On Working Drawings

Beginners in drafting must know how to draw certain lines in order to make working drawings. See Fig. 2-8.

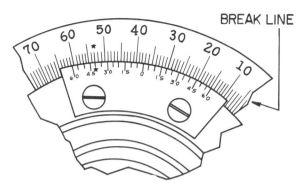

BREAK LINE

Fig. 2-9.   Break lines show that a part of a surface has been removed.

A **visible line** is a thick line used to show all edges that can be seen. See Figs. 2-5 and 2-8.

A **hidden line,** sometimes called an **invisible edge** or a **dotted line,** is made of 1/8″ dashes 1/16″ apart (3 mm dashes 1.5 mm apart). It is used to show hidden edges, as if you could look right through the object. See Figs. 2-4 and 2-8.

An **extension line** is a thin line. It is drawn from the edge from which the measurement is to be made. Note in Fig. 2-5 that the extension line does not touch the object. It should be about 1/16″ (1.5 mm) from the object and extend about 1/8″ (3 mm) past the arrowhead.

A **dimension line** is also a thin line. It is drawn between the extension lines about 3/8″ (9 mm) from the object. The dimension is in the opening in the dimension line. See Figs. 2-5 and 2-8.

Centerlines, Figs. 2-5 and 2-8, locate the centers of circles or arcs. They are the foundation lines for measuring. They must be drawn before the circle or arc is drawn. The centerline is also used to show the axis of an object and to locate slots. A centerline is a thin line, a dash, and a thin line. It is made horizontally and vertically through the center of every circle and arc. The dashes should cross at the center of the circle or arc. Centerlines also show the centers of slots and grooves. See Fig. 2-5.

Bending lines are shown in Fig. 2-8. A small circle is drawn by hand at each end of the line.

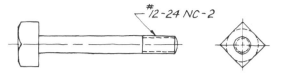

Fig. 2-10.   Sketch of a bolt.

Fig. 2-11.   Sketching a line near edge of the paper.

A **break line** is a wavy line. It is used to show that a part is broken off. See Fig. 2-9.

SKETCHING

Often, the step to a better job is in learning to read drawings as well as make them. The worker must not only know how to read the language of the industrial world but also how to write it. Sometimes a part for a machine must be made when there is no time for a drafter to make a drawing. In such cases, the worker must make a sketch or freehand drawing in the shop. With just pencil and paper, the worker can quickly make a working drawing that will fill the need. A sketch of a bolt is shown in Fig. 2-10. Figures 2-11 through 2-17 show ways to sketch lines and circles.

Sketches are valuable. They show ideas and dimensions of a part. The beginner should practice making clean sketches that give all the information needed. The sketches must be read easily by others.

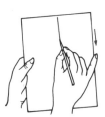

Fig. 2-12. Sketching a line near center of the paper.

Fig. 2-15. Sketching a small circle with two pencils.

Fig. 2-13. Sketching a line along upper edge of the paper.

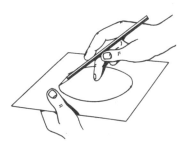

Fig. 2-16. Sketching a large circle with two pencils.

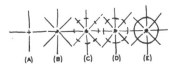

(A)   (B)   (C)   (D)   (E)

Fig. 2-14. Steps in sketching a circle.

Fig. 2-17. Sketching a circle using pencil and middle finger.

METRIC DIMENSIONING

The United States is rapidly changing to the SI metric system of measurements. Until this change is complete, many working drawings need both metric and U.S. customary dimensions. Figure 2-18 shows some of the common ways to dual dimension. When using a working drawing with dual dimensions, follow **either** the metric or U.S. customary measurements entirely. Do not mix the two systems. Otherwise, the parts may not fit together correctly.

The metric system is covered in more detail in Chapter 3. Refer to it if you have any questions about metric conversion.

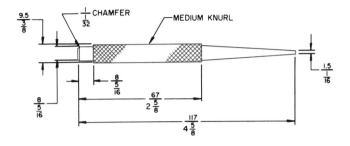

Fig. 2-18. Example of dual dimensioning.

PROJECT IDEAS

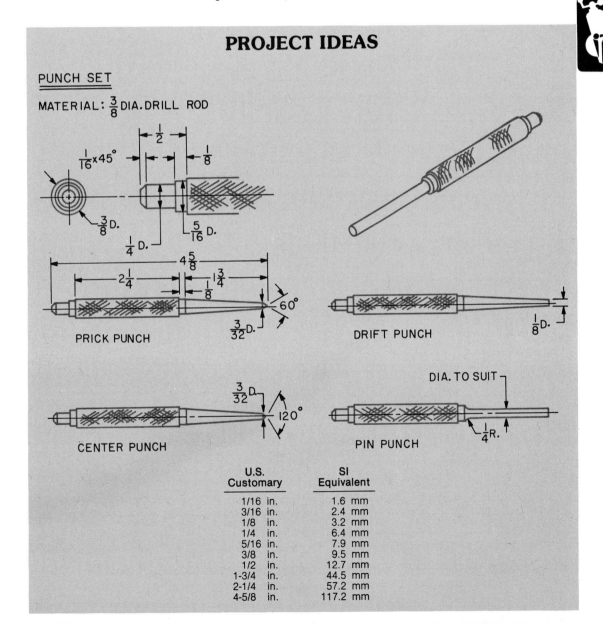

PUNCH SET

MATERIAL: $\frac{3}{8}$ DIA. DRILL ROD

PRICK PUNCH

DRIFT PUNCH

CENTER PUNCH

PIN PUNCH

U.S. Customary	SI Equivalent
1/16 in.	1.6 mm
3/16 in.	2.4 mm
1/8 in.	3.2 mm
1/4 in.	6.4 mm
5/16 in.	7.9 mm
3/8 in.	9.5 mm
1/2 in.	12.7 mm
1-3/4 in.	44.5 mm
2-1/4 in.	57.2 mm
4-5/8 in.	117.2 mm

COLD CHISEL

MATERIAL: $\frac{7}{16}$ HEXAGON OR
OCTAGON TOOL STEEL

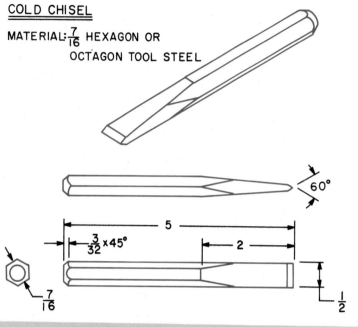

U.S. Customary		SI Equivalent
3/32	in.	2.4 mm
7/16	in.	11.1 mm
1/2	in.	12.7 mm
2	in.	50.8 mm
5	in.	127.0 mm

60°

5

$\frac{3}{32}$ x 45°

2

$\frac{7}{16}$

$\frac{1}{2}$

U.S. Customary		SI Equivalent
1/8	in.	3.2 mm
3/8	in.	9.5 mm
1/2	in.	12.7 mm
3/4	in.	19.1 mm
1	in.	25.4 mm
1-1/4	in.	31.7 mm
1-1/2	in.	38.0 mm
2-1/2	in.	63.5 mm
14-9/16	in.	369.9 mm

GARDEN TROWEL

MATERIAL: 18 GAGE HOT OR COLD FINISHED STEEL FOR TROWEL BODY

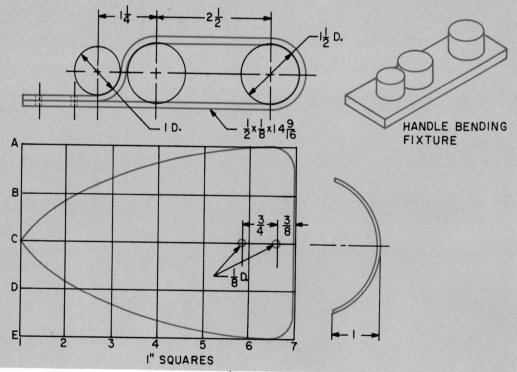

$1\frac{1}{4}$

$2\frac{1}{2}$

$1\frac{1}{2}$ D.

1 D.

$\frac{1}{2}$ x $\frac{1}{8}$ x 14 $\frac{9}{16}$

HANDLE BENDING
FIXTURE

$\frac{3}{4}$

$\frac{3}{8}$

$\frac{1}{8}$ D.

1

A
B
C
D
E

2 3 4 5 6 7

I" SQUARES

PLANTER

MATERIAL: 18 GA. COPPER, BRASS OR
             GALVANIZED

TYPICAL CORNER DETAIL-SOLDER

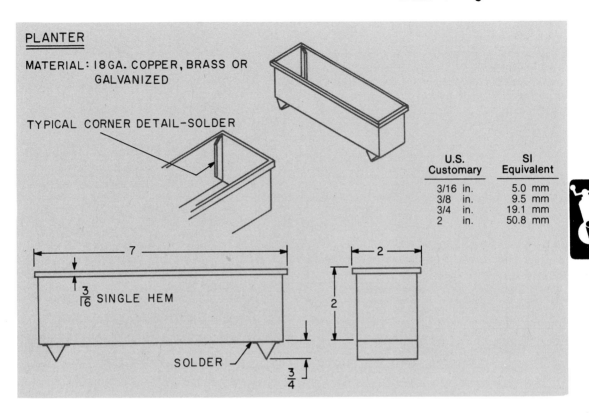

U.S. Customary	SI Equivalent
3/16 in.	5.0 mm
3/8 in.	9.5 mm
3/4 in.	19.1 mm
2 in.	50.8 mm

7

$\frac{3}{16}$ SINGLE HEM

2

2

SOLDER

$\frac{3}{4}$

PENDANTS

MATERIAL: ALUMINUM, BRASS,
          COPPER, STAINLESS
          STEEL

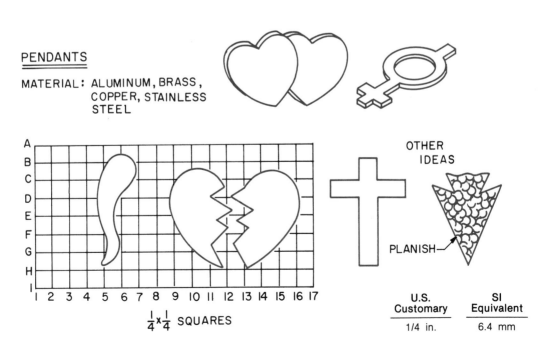

OTHER IDEAS

PLANISH—

A B C D E F G H I

1 2 3 4 5 6 7 8 9 10 11 12 13 14 15 16 17

$\frac{1}{4} \times \frac{1}{4}$ SQUARES

U.S. Customary	SI Equivalent
1/4 in.	6.4 mm

MAIL BOX

MAKE A MAIL BOX. GET IDEAS FROM MAIL
ORDER CATALOGS. USE SHEET METAL,
BRASS, ALUMINUM OR GALVANIZED SHEET.
JOIN SEAMS BY SPOT WELDING OR SOLDER-
ING.

THE DESIGN MAYBE

VERTICAL TYPE

HORIZONTAL TYPE

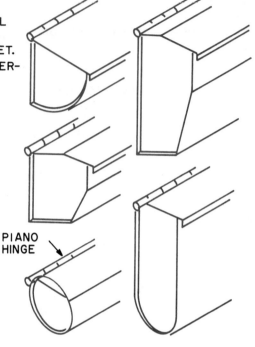

PIANO
HINGE

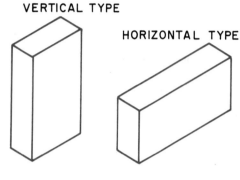

RANCH CHIME

MATERIAL : HOT FINISHED MILD STEEL

U.S. Customary	SI Equivalent
3/16 in.	5.0 mm
1/4 in.	6.4 mm
1/2 in.	12.7 mm
5/8 in.	15.9 mm
3/4 in.	19.1 mm
1 in.	25.4 mm
1-1/4 in.	31.7 mm
1-1/2 in.	38.0 mm
8 in.	203.2 mm
9-1/2 in.	241.3 mm
10 in.	254.0 mm
12 in.	304.8 mm

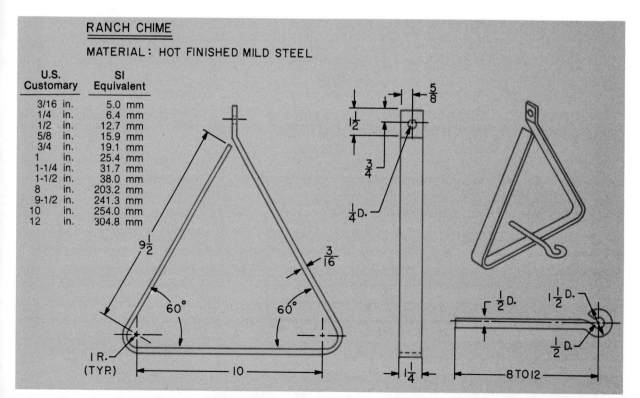

BRACELET

MATERIAL: 16-18 GA. STERLING, NICKEL, ALUMINUM OR BRASS

ALTERNATE DESIGNS

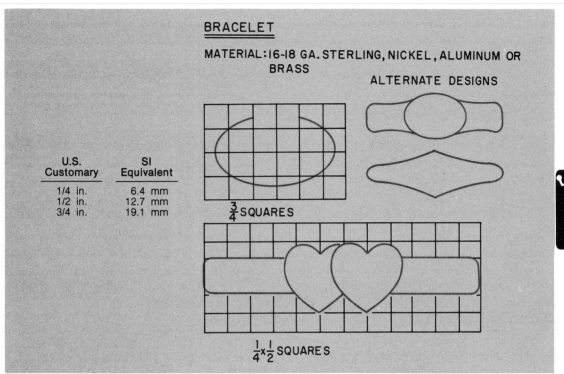

U.S. Customary	SI Equivalent
1/4 in.	6.4 mm
1/2 in.	12.7 mm
3/4 in.	19.1 mm

$\frac{3}{4}$ SQUARES

$\frac{1}{4} \times \frac{1}{2}$ SQUARES

BOTTLE OPENER

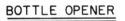

MATERIAL: $\frac{1}{8}$ - $\frac{3}{16}$ HARD BRASS OR MILD STEEL

U.S. Customary	SI Equivalent
1/8 in.	3.2 mm
3/16 in.	4.8 mm
1/4 in.	6.4 mm
3/4 in.	19.1 mm
1-3/16 in.	30.2 mm

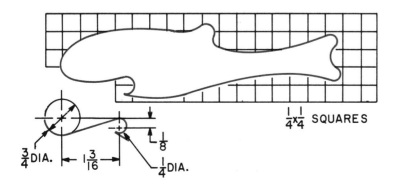

$\frac{1}{4} \times \frac{1}{4}$ SQUARES

$\frac{3}{4}$ DIA. $1\frac{3}{16}$ $\frac{1}{8}$ $\frac{1}{4}$ DIA.

Selecting, Measuring, Laying Out   Chapter **3**

LAYING OUT

Laying out is the marking of lines, circles, and arcs on metal surfaces. The worker takes information from a working drawing and transfers it to metal surfaces. The layout shows the location and amount of metal to be cut away. In many ways, laying out on metal is the same as making a mechanical drawing on paper.

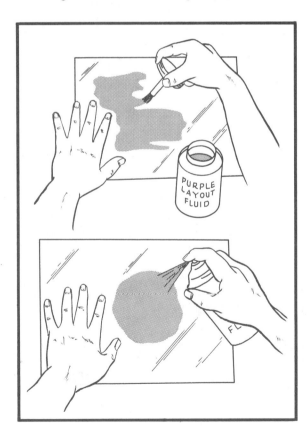

Fig. 3-1.   Metal is colored with a layout fluid.

COLORING METAL FOR LAYOUT

The first step in layout work is to color the surface upon which the lines are to be made. Rough surfaces may be covered with white chalk or a white paint. The chalk should be rubbed into the metal with the fingers until smooth.

Iron and steel surfaces that are smooth and bright may be coated with layout fluid. The metal is first wiped clean. Then the fluid is put on with a brush or sprayed on, Fig. 3-1. It dries quickly. Use steel wool or alcohol to remove the dried layout fluid.

SCRIBER

You can scribe or scratch lines on metal by using a tool called the **scriber.** This is a piece of hardened steel about 6″ to 10″ (152 to 254 mm) long. It is pointed on one or both ends like a needle, Fig. 3-2. The bent end is used to scratch lines in places where the straight end cannot reach. To use the scriber, hold it as you would a pencil. Sharpen the points on an oilstone.

After the layout fluid has dried on the metal surface, you can begin making the layout. To draw a straight line, place the steel rule,

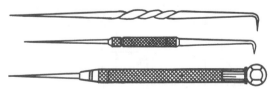

Fig. 3-2.   Scribers.

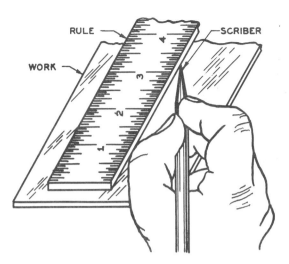

Fig. 3-3.   Slant the scriber so the point follows the lower edge of the rule.

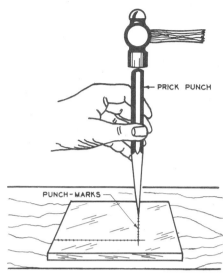

Fig. 3-5.   Prick punching a line.

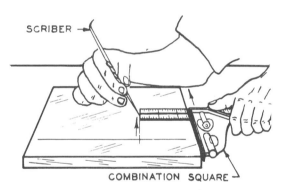

Fig. 3-4.   Scribing a line, using a combination square.

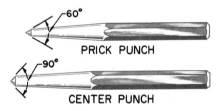

Fig. 3-6.   The center punch has a blunter point than the prick punch.

square, or bevel protractor in the correct position. Hold it against the work with the left hand. (If you are left handed, hold it with the right hand.) Hold the scriber in the other hand. Lean it to one side so that the point will draw along the lower edge of the rule. See Figs. 3-3 and 3-4. Scratch one line. Be sure your scriber is sharp.

PRICK PUNCH

The coloring and the scribed lines of a layout wear off in the handling of the work. The lines should be prick punched to make them last longer. See Fig. 3-5. Place the point of the prick punch exactly on the line. Hold it squarely on the metal surface and strike lightly with the hammer. The punch marks should be made closer together on curved lines than on straight lines.

CENTER PUNCH

The center punch looks like a prick punch, Fig. 3-6. It is usually larger than the prick punch. The prick punch has a sharper point. Both are made of hardened steel.

The center punch is used only to make the prick punch marks larger at the centers of holes. This is so drilling can start easily and correctly.

TEMPLATE

A template, also spelled templet, is a pattern. It is used to mark the shape of pieces of work, mark holes, and so on. The template is usually made of plastic or sheet metal. You can use it to lay out many duplicate pieces. See Fig. 3-7. Lay the template on the work. Mark lines and circles with a scriber. Using a template requires fewer layout tools. It also saves time because there is less measuring.

LAYING OUT CIRCLES AND ARCS

Divider

Dividers are used to scribe circles and parts of circles to lay off distances and to measure distances. The divider is a two-legged steel instrument with hardened points, Fig. 3-8. Its size is measured by the maximum distance it can be opened between the two points. Thus, a 4″ (102 mm) divider opens 4″ between the points. A 6″ (152 mm) divider opens 6″ between the points, and so on. Both points of the divider should be even in length. Sharpen them on an oilstone.

Setting A Divider

To make a circle, set the divider to the size of the radius which is one-half of the diameter. For example, if the circle is to be 4″ (102 mm) in diameter, the divider should be set at 2″ (51 mm). Setting a divider to a certain size is shown in Fig. 3-9. Place one point of the divider into one of the lines of the steel rule. Then move the other point until it exactly splits the other line at which the divider is to be set. Being able to feel the V-shape of the lines helps you set the divider points correctly. Handle the divider carefully to avoid springing.

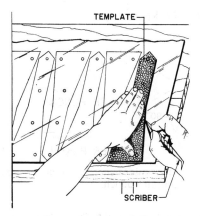

Fig. 3-7.   Laying out work with a template.

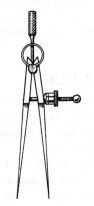

Fig. 3-8.   Divider.

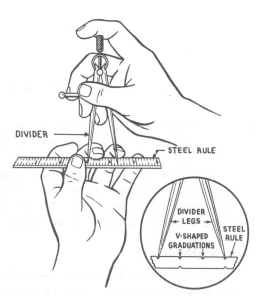

Fig. 3-9.   Setting the divider.

MEASURING PROCESSES

Using the Steel Rule

The steel rule, also called **machinist's rule,** is made in many thicknesses, widths, and lengths. Because a steel rule is used to measure, it should be handled with care. Edges and corners must not become nicked or worn round.

The edges of steel rules are divided by fine lines into **millimeters.** U.S. customary rules divided into inches are also commonly used.

To measure with a steel rule, stand the rule up on its edge on the work. The lines on the rule should touch the work, Fig. 3-10. The division line on the rule has a certain thickness. Always measure to the center of the line. Measure from the 1″ or 10 mm mark because the end of the rule may be worn.

Combination Set

The combination set, Fig. 3-11, is the most commonly used set of tools in the machine shop. The set includes a square head, center head, bevel protractor, spirit level, steel rule, and scriber. The rule or blade may be fastened quickly to each of the first three. The beginner should ask how this is done so that the small parts will not be lost or damaged. Figures 3-12 and 3-13 show ways that the steel rule can be used when the square head, bevel protractor, or center head are fastened to it.

Combination Square

The combination square has many uses. Note that 45° and 90° angles can be measured with it, Fig. 3-12. If the work has one straight edge, parallel lines and perpendicular lines may be laid out. See Fig. 3-13.

MICROMETERS

Extremely fine measurements can be made by using the micrometer, Fig. 3-14. Exactness in measuring depends on a sense of touch or feel.

READING A MICROMETER

All micrometers are read alike. The end of the spindle, inside the thimble, is called the **screw spindle.** The sleeve is fastened to the end of the screw. The screw has 40 threads to an inch. That is, the screw must turn 40 times to

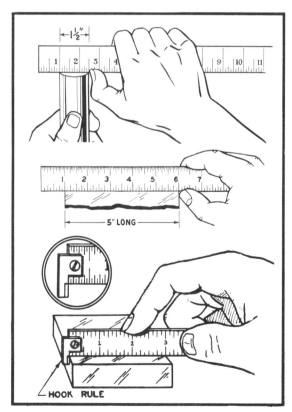

Fig. 3-10. Measuring with edge of a steel rule.

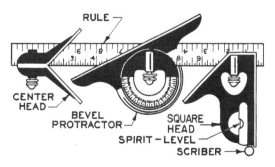

Fig. 3-11. Combination set having U.S. customary measurements.

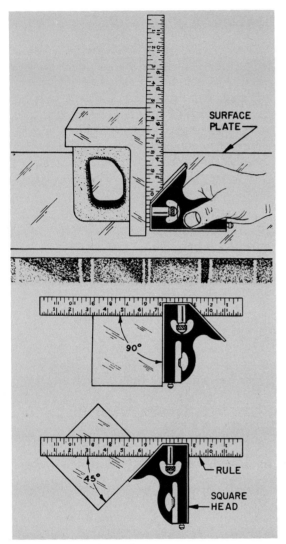

Fig. 3-12. Uses of a combination square.

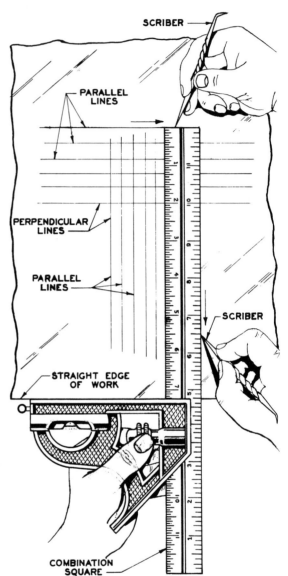

Fig. 3-13. Laying out parallel and perpendicular lines with a combination square when the work has only one straight edge.

move 1 inch. Thus, each turn of the screw equals 1/40". The micrometer is read in thousandths of an inch instead of 40ths of an inch. Therefore, 1/40 of an inch must be changed to thousandths of an inch. This is done by dividing the numerator by the denominator:

$$40 \overline{)1.000} \quad .025$$

There are also 40 lines to an inch on the sleeve. This is the same as the number of threads on the screw. These lines show how

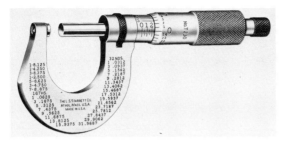

Fig. 3-14. Micrometers are used for accurate measurements. This one has U.S. customary measurements.

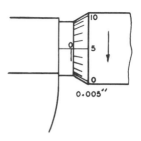

Fig. 3-16. Five thousandths of an inch (.005″).

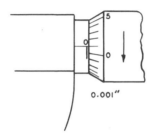

Fig. 3-15. One thousandth of an inch (.001″).

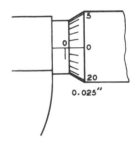

Fig. 3-17. Twenty-five thousandths of an inch (.025″).

many times the screw has turned. Each turn equals .025″. If one turn of the screw equals .025″, then 1/25 of a turn equals 1/25 of .025″, or .001″. Thus, by dividing the edge of the thimble into 25 parts, it is possible to make exactly 1/25 of a turn which is .001″. Or, 2/25 of a turn is .002″, etc. This makes it possible to measure in thousandths of an inch. One-half and quarters of a thousandth can be judged as nearly as possible.

Marks on the Sleeve and Thimble

Turn the thimble until the **0 mark** on the thimble and the **0 mark** on the sleeve come together. This gives the smallest size that the micrometer will measure. On a 1″ micrometer it is 0. On a 2″ micrometer it is 1″. On a 3″ micrometer it is 2″.

The marks on the thimble are .001″ each. Turn the thimble to the next line on the thimble turning in the direction of the arrow, Fig. 3-15.

On a 1″ micrometer, the spindle will be .001″ from the anvil. Turn the thimble to the line marked 5 on the thimble, Fig. 3-16. The spindle will be .005″ from the anvil.

Note that one complete turn of the thimble is .025″ on the sleeve, Fig. 3-17. For each turn of the thimble, the thimble moves over one more mark on the sleeve. This means that each mark on the sleeve is .025″. Every fourth line on the sleeve is a little longer that the others and is stamped 1, 2, 3, etc., which stands for .100″, .200″, .300″, etc. The micrometer is set at .100″ in Fig. 3-18.

To find out how much the micrometer is opened (the distance between the anvil and the spindle), the marks on the sleeve may be read like any ordinary rule. Refer back to Fig. 3-14. Remember that the numbers 1, 2, 3, 4, etc., mean .100″, .200″, .300″, .400″, etc. To this, add the thousandths that show on the thimble. For example, the readings in Fig. 3-19 are:

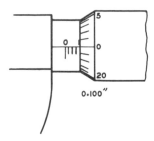

Fig. 3-18. One hundred thousandths of an inch (.100″).

(A) .200″ even
(B) .250″ (.200″ + .025″ + .025″
    = .250″)
(C) .562″ (.500″ + .050″ + .012″
    = .562″)
(D) .787½″ (.700″ + .075″ + .012½″-
    = .787½″ or .7875″)

Be sure to add correctly.

Reading a Ten-Thousandth Micrometer

Some micrometers have a **vernier** which is 10 divisions on the back of the sleeve. A vernier micrometer can be read to a ten-thousandth of an inch (1/10000″ or .0001″). Again, each mark on the thimble is .001″. The lines of the vernier are numbered 0, 1, 2, 3, 4, 5, 6, 7, 8, 9, 0. See Fig. 3-20. These lines have the same space as 9 divisions on the thimble.

To read the vernier micrometer, first read the thousandths as on any micrometer. Suppose that this number is between .275 and .276, as in Fig. 3-20. To find the fourth decimal place, find the line on the vernier that matches exactly a line on the thimble. In this case, it is the line 4. This number 4 means 4 ten-thousandths inches (.0004″) and added to the .275″ gives the fourth decimal place. Thus, the complete reading is .2754″ (.275″ + .0004″ = .2754″).

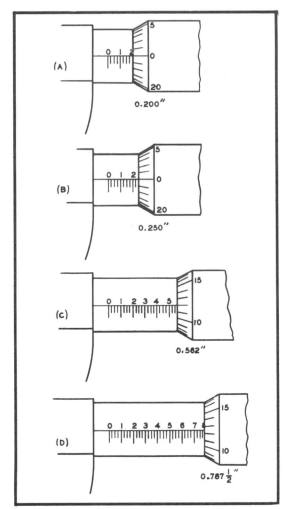

Fig. 3-19. Reading a micrometer.

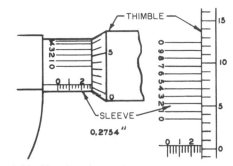

Fig. 3-20. Vernier micrometer.

DECIMAL EQUIVALENTS

You must know how to convert common fractions to decimal equivalents in order to read

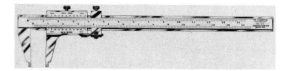

Fig. 3-21. The vernier caliper makes measurements to one-thousandth of an inch. Also, it can take both inside and outside measurements.

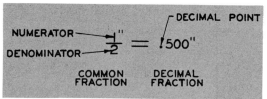

Fig. 3-22. Decimal equivalent.

and use tools like micrometers. See Fig. 3-21. Measurements made by micrometers and verniers are in decimal fractions. Decimal fractions are decimal equivalents of common fractions. They are obtained by dividing the numerator of a common fraction by its denominator, as ½ = 1 ÷ 2, or

$$\begin{array}{r} .5 \\ 2\overline{)1.0} \end{array}$$

English micrometers and verniers are both read in thousandths of an inch. This is three places to the right of the decimal point (.001″, .003″). All decimal fractions must also be carried out to three places. Thus, ½″ = .500. See Fig. 3-22.

The decimal equivalent of any fraction is found in the same way as above. Two other examples follow:

1. 3/8″ = 3 ÷ 8 =

$$\begin{array}{r} .375 \\ 8\overline{)3.000} \\ 2\ 4 \\ \hline 60 \\ 56 \\ \hline 40 \\ 40 \end{array}$$

The decimal equivalent of 3/8″ is therefore .375″. It is read three hundred seventy-five thousandths.

2. 9/16″ = 9 ÷ 16 =

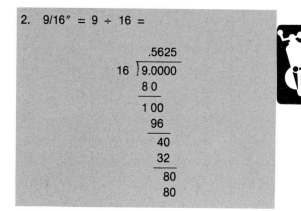

$$\begin{array}{r} .5625 \\ 16\overline{)9.0000} \\ 8\ 0 \\ \hline 1\ 00 \\ 96 \\ \hline 40 \\ 32 \\ \hline 80 \\ 80 \end{array}$$

Therefore, .5625″ is the decimal equivalent of 9/16″. It is read five hundred sixty-two and one-half thousandths or five hundred sixty-two and five ten-thousandths.

When parts are to be made to very exact sizes, decimal fractions are used on working drawings instead of common fractions. When common fractions appear on working drawings of metal parts, the actual size may vary 1/64″ either way from the stated size. However, when decimal fractions are used, the size can vary only .005″ either way from the stated size. The decimal fraction for 1/64″ is .0156″.

To save time, decimal equivalents are usually stamped on the frame of the micrometer. The worker should memorize the decimal equivalents of 1/2″, 1/4″, 1/8″, 1/16″, 1/32″, and 1/64″. If these are known, most of the decimal equivalents which must be used can be figured out.

DECIMAL RULE

The inch on a decimal rule is divided into 10 and 100 parts. See Fig. 3-33. Quarters,

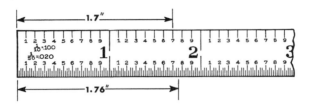

Fig. 3-23. Decimal rule.

eighths, sixteenths, and so on are not used. By using this rule, you do not need to change from a common fraction to a decimal fraction. Measurements are made quicker with this rule when you need decimal dimensions. The smallest divisions on some of these rules are 50 parts to an inch instead of 100 so that they can be read easily.

SI METRIC MEASUREMENTS

The measuring system used in the United States is different from that used in most of the other countries of the world. There is an increasing amount of interchange of tools, material, products, and even skilled workers among the countries of the world. Industrial firms of the United States have begun to convert to the metric system or International System of Units (SI).

The familiar units of measure such as the inch, foot, yard, and mile are not meaningful to most of the world's population. Most other countries express length in terms of a basic unit known as the meter. For example, one meter equals 39.37 inches, 3.2808 feet, 1.0936 yards, and 1000 meters or 1 kilometer equals 0.62137 mile. However, in countries using the meter as the base unit, parts of and multiples of the meter are used. When the meter is divided by 10, each of the 10 parts is called a decimeter. When the decimeter is divided by 10, each of the 10 parts is referred to as a centimeter. Each centimeter can be divided by 10 to have units referred to as millimeters. (1/10 (0.1) meter = decimeter; 1/100 (0.01) meter = centimeter; 1/1000 (0.001) meter = millimeter.)

Conversion Tables

Dimensions in inches can be converted to dimensions in millimeters by using the tables here. Figure 3-28 lists fractions of an inch, their decimal equivalent in inches, and their equivalent in millimeters. With this table, the metric equivalent of a common fraction such as for example 5/16" can quickly be found to be 7.938 mm. (In practice, this would probably be rounded off to 8 mm.)

Figure 3-29 converts decimal parts of an inch to millimeters. If you want the metric equivalent of a decimal figure such as .835 inches, find it by using the following procedure:

0.8	in.	=	20.32 mm
0.03	in.	=	0.762 mm
0.005	in.	=	0.127 mm
0.835	in.	=	21.209 mm

By using Figs. 3-28 and 3-29 together, you can figure the metric equivalent of any measurement in inches.

Fig. 3-24
SI Base Units

Quantity	Unit	Symbol
Length	Meter	m
Mass	Kilogram	kg
Time	Second	s
Electric Current	Ampere	A
Temperature	Kelvin	K
Amount of Substance	Mole	mol
Luminous Intensity	Candela	cd

LENGTH

U.S. to Metric	Metric to U.S.
1 inch = 25.40 millimeters	1 millimeter = 0.03937 inch
1 inch = 2.540 centimeters	1 centimeter = 0.3937 inch
1 foot = 30.480 centimeters	1 meter = 39.97 inches
1 foot = 0.3048 meter	1 meter = 3.2808 feet
1 yard = 91.440 centimeters	1 meter = 1.0936 yards
1 mile = 1.609 kilometers	1 kilometer = 0.62137 mile

AREA

U.S. to Metric	Metric to U.S.
1 sq. inch = 645.16 sq. millimeters	1 sq. millimeter = 0.00155 sq. inch
1 sq. inch = 6.4515 sq. centimeters	1 sq. centimeter = 0.1550 sq. inch
1 sq. foot = 929.03 sq. centimeters	
1 sq. foot = 0.0929 sq.meter	1 sq. meter = 10.764 sq. feet
1 sq. yard = 0.836 sq. meter	1 sq. meter = 1.196 sq. yards
1 acre = 0.4047 sq. hectometer	1 sq. hectometer = 2.471 acres
1 acre = 0.4047 hectare	1 hectare = 2.471 acres
1 sq. mile = 2.59 sq. kilometers	1 sq. kilometer = 0.386 sq. mile

MASS (Weight)

U.S. to Metric	Metric to U.S.
1 ounce (dry) = 28.35 grams	1 gram = 0.03527 ounce
1 pound = 0.4536 kilogram	1 kilogram = 2.2046 pounds
1 short ton (2000 lb.) = 907.2 kilograms	1 metric ton = 2204.6 pounds
1 short ton (2000 lb.) = 0.9072 metric ton	1 metric ton = 1.102 tons (short)

VOLUME (Capacity)

U.S. to Metric	Metric to U.S.
1 fluid ounce = 2.957 centiliters	1 centiliter = 10 cm³*
= 29.57 cm³*	= 0.338 fluid ounce
1 pint (liq.) = 4.732 dekaliters	1 dekaliter = 100 cm³*
= 473.2 cm³*	= 0.0528 pint (liq.)
1 quart (liq.) = 0.9463 liters	1 liter = dm³**
= 0.9463 cm³*	= 0.26417 gallon (liq.)

*cubic centimeter
**cubic decimeter

Fig. 3-26.   Precision 15 cm scale with 1 mm and 0.5 mm graduations.

Fig. 3-27. Comparison between 1 meter and 1 yard.

Fraction	Inches	Millimeters	Fraction	Inches	Millimeters
1/64	0.016	0.397	33/64	0.516	13.097
1/32	0.031	0.794	17/32	0.531	13.494
3/64	0.047	1.191	35/64	0.547	13.891
1/16	0.063	1.588	9/16	0.563	14.288
5/64	0.078	1.984	37/64	0.578	14.684
3/32	0.094	2.381	19/32	0.594	15.081
7/64	0.109	2.788	39/64	0.609	15.478
1/8	0.125	3.175	5/8	0.625	15.875
9/64	0.141	3.572	41/64	0.641	16.272
5/32	0.156	3.969	21/32	0.656	16.669
11/64	0.172	4.366	43/64	0.672	17.066
3/16	0.186	4.763	11/16	0.688	17.463
13/64	0.203	5.159	45/64	0.703	17.859
7/32	0.219	5.556	23/32	0.719	18.256
15/64	0.234	5.953	47/64	0.734	18.653
1/4	0.250	6.350	3/4	0.750	19.050
17/64	0.266	6.747	49/64	0.766	19.447
9/32	0.281	7.144	25/32	0.781	19.844
19/64	0.297	7.541	51/64	0.797	20.241
5/16	0.313	7.938	13/16	0.813	20.638
21/64	0.328	8.334	53/64	0.828	21.034
11/32	0.344	8.731	27/32	0.844	21.431
23/64	0.359	9.128	55/64	0.859	21.828
3/8	0.375	9.525	7/8	0.875	22.225
25/64	0.391	9.922	57/64	0.891	22.622
13/32	0.406	10.319	29/32	0.906	23.019
27/64	0.422	10.716	59/64	0.922	23.416
7/16	0.438	11.113	15/16	0.938	23.813
29/64	0.453	11.509	61/64	0.953	24.209
15/32	0.469	11.906	31/32	0.969	24.606
31/64	0.484	12.303	63/64	0.984	25.003
1/2	0.500	12.700	1	1.000	25.400

Fig. 3-29
Conversion Table
Decimal Parts of an Inch to Millimeters

Inches	Millimeters	Inches	Millimeters	Inches	Millimeters
0.001	0.025	0.01	0.254	0.1	2.54
0.002	0.051	0.02	0.508	0.2	5.08
0.003	0.076	0.03	0.762	0.3	7.62
0.004	0.102	0.04	1.016	0.4	10.16
0.005	0.127	0.05	1.270	0.5	12.70
0.006	0.152	0.06	1.524	0.6	15.24
0.007	0.178	0.07	1.778	0.7	17.78
0.008	0.203	0.08	2.032	0.8	20.32
0.009	0.229	0.09	2.286	0.9	22.86

Chapter **4**

CUTTING AND SHAPING

Bench metalworking usually involves hand tools and simple machine processes. This chapter describes processes used to shape and cut metal. These are some of the more common shaping and cutting processes:

1. Sawing
2. Chiseling
3. Filing
4. Drilling
5. Abrading

SAWING BY HAND

A hack saw is the most common hand tool used to cut metal to length. See Fig. 4-1. Many types of blades are available. They have different-sized teeth for cutting different kinds and shapes of metal.

Blade Selection

Hand hacksaw blades are made of thin high-grade steel that has been hardened and tempered. Some blades are all hard which makes them quite brittle. Other kinds of blades have hardened teeth and a softer back. These are classed as flexible blades. The softer back makes the blade springy and less likely to break. Blades are available in several kinds of material. They include carbon steel, molybdenum alloy steel, tungsten alloy steel, molybdenum high-speed steel, and tungsten high-speed steel.

Number of Teeth Per Inch

The number of teeth per inch varies with the type of blade and the purpose it serves. A blade always has one more point than the number of complete teeth. See Fig. 4-2.

a. **14 teeth per inch:** for cutting soft steel, aluminum, brass, bronze, copper alloys. Cuts other materials 1″ or more in thickness.

b. **18 teeth per inch:** for cutting machine steel, angle iron, drill rod, tool steel, aluminum, copper alloys, and other materials 1/4″ to 1″ in thickness. For general-purpose work.

c. **24 teeth per inch:** for cutting materials 1/16″ to 1/4″ thickness, such as iron pipe, metal conduits, and light angle iron.

d. **32 teeth per inch:** for cutting materials up to 1/16″ thickness. Cuts sheet metals, thin wall tubing, and thin angles or channels.

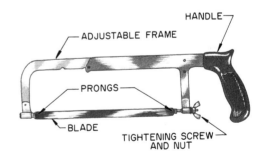

Fig. 4-1.   Parts of the hand hacksaw.

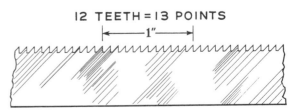

Fig. 4-2.   Points per inch on the saw blade.

Replacing the Blade

When putting a new blade in the hand hacksaw, place it so that the teeth point away from the handle. Fasten one end of the blade to the hook at one end of the frame. Fasten the other end of the blade over the hook at the opposite end of the frame, Fig. 4-3. Strain the blade well as you tighten the tightening screw. A loose blade makes a crooked cut and is likely to break.

CUTTING STROKE

To begin a cut in the metal, notch the starting place with a file. This makes the starting saw strokes easier. Place the saw on the work and begin with a backward stroke. Press down on the forward stroke and lift a little on the return stroke. The blade cuts only on the forward stroke. The first few strokes should be short ones with only a little pressure. When the saw kerf is deep enough that the blade will not jump out, increase the stroke to the full blade length. Add more pressure. Fig. 4-4. Tighten the blade again after a few strokes since it will stretch when it becomes warm.

COPING SAW

Curved outlines are cut with a coping saw or with a jeweler's saw (also called a piercing saw), Fig. 4-5. Irregular holes can also be cut or pierced with these saws.

Metal-cutting blades for the jeweler's saw have fine teeth and must be very hard in order to cut metal. They are 5″ long and have from 32 to 76 teeth per inch. The teeth of the blade should point toward the handle.

The work should be held on a board with a V-shaped notch. Lay the board on the edge of the bench and hold down with your hand or with a clamp. Use your right hand to saw (or left if you're left-handed), Fig. 4-6. The cutting stroke is downward. For internal cuts, drill a hole through the metal and put the blade through the hole. Then fasten the blade to the saw frame.

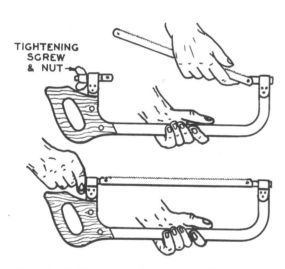

TIGHTENING SCREW & NUT →

Fig. 4-3.   Putting a new blade in the saw frame.

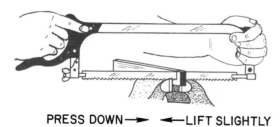

PRESS DOWN →   ← LIFT SLIGHTLY

Fig. 4-4.   Press down on forward strokes of hacksaw. Lift slightly on return stroke.

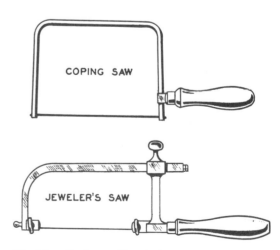

COPING SAW

JEWELER'S SAW

Fig. 4-5.   Coping and jeweler's saws.

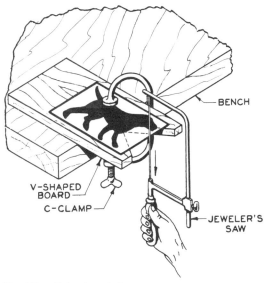

Fig. 4-6.   Using jeweler's saw.

A. Power hacksaw

SAWING BY MACHINE

Three common types of power sawing machines are used to saw metals. They are (1) power hacksaw, (2) vertical band saw, and (3) horizontal band saw.

Power Hacksaw

The power hacksaw saws all kinds of metal, except hardened steel. See **A** in Fig. 4-7. The blade must always be harder than the material to be cut. The frame and blade move forward and backward. The saw is driven by an electric motor.

Vertical Band Saw

A vertical band saw, **B** in Fig. 4-7, is also called a **contouring machine.** Its blade runs in one direction. The blade of the vertical band saw is in a vertical position. A blade shear and a blade welder are often mounted on the saw for cutting and welding band saw blades. Band saws are also made that can be changed to either a horizontal or vertical type band saw.

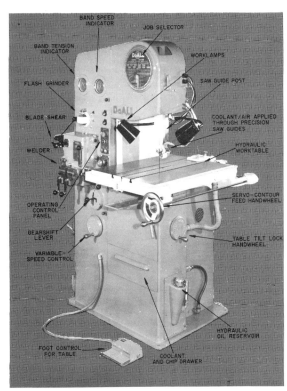

B. Vertical band saw

Fig. 4-7.   Power Sawing Machines

Making Cuts

Vertical band saws may be used to make straight line cuts, angular cuts, or curved line cuts. Curved line cuts are called **contour cuts**. Hence, vertical band saws are also called **contouring machines**. The saw table may be tilted at any desired angle up to 45° for making angular cuts.

To make internal contour cuts, you must drill a hole in the workpiece first. The blade is then cut with the blade shear. It is inserted through the drilled hole in the workpiece and rewelded with the blade welder. Next, the blade is installed on the machine and properly tensioned. You can now make the contour cut. When the work is done, the blade must again be removed from the machine and sheared. The finished workpiece can then be removed.

BAND SAW CUTTING SPEEDS

The cutting speed for band saws may be varied in several ways. This depends on the type of motor drive system on the machine. The drive system of many vertical band saws have variable speeds. With this type of drive, the machine may be changed to any desired speed within its range. However, with this type of drive system, the speed can be changed only while the machine is running.

Recommended cutting speeds are based on these factors:

1. Kind of material being cut.
2. Hardness of the material.
3. Thickness of the material.
4. Whether the cutting is wet or dry.

Slower cutting speeds are used when harder metals are cut. They are also used for cutting thick materials rather than thinner ones. Higher cutting speeds may be used for wet cutting rather than dry cutting.

Figure 4-8 suggests average speeds for cutting material ½" to 1" thickness with either a horizontal or vertical band saw. Speeds are expressed in surface feet per minute (sfpm) or meters per minute.

Fig. 4-8
Cutting Speeds (sfpm) for Band Saws

Material	Cutting Speed (sfm)	
	Dry	Wet
Alloy Steel (tough)	125	175
Aluminum	250	800
Bakelite	300	
Brass (soft)	500	800
Brass (hard)	200	300
Bronze	200	300
Copper	250	400
Drill Rod (annealed)	75	125
Gray Cast Iron (soft)	125	
Hard Rubber	200	
High-Speed Steel	50	75
Low-Carbon Steel	125	175
Malleable Iron	125	175
Medium-Carbon Steel	100	150

The cutting speeds in Fig. 4-8 may be increased about 25% for cutting materials ¼" (6 mm) or less in thickness. They should be decreased by about 25% for materials which are 2" (50 mm) or more in thickness.

BAND SAW BLADE SELECTION

Blade Material

Metal-cutting band saw blades are made from different steels. They may be high-carbon steel, special alloy steel, and high-speed steel. The alloy steel blades and high-speed steel blades are designed for heavy-duty production work. The high-carbon steel blades have hardened teeth and a softer flexible back. They often cost the least. Carbon steel blades satisfy many needs. They are widely used on both horizontal and vertical machines in school shops, small machine shops, and maintenance machine shops.

Blade Width

Blades are available in the widths shown in Fig. 4-9. A narrow width blade cuts a smaller

Fig. 4-9
Metal Cutting Band Saw Blade Sizes

Width	Thickness	Teeth Per Inch
3/32	0.025	18
1/8	0.025	14-18-24
3/16	0.025	10-14-18
1/4	0.025	10-14-18-24
3/8	0.025	8-10-14-18
1/2	0.025	6-8-10-14-18-24
5/8	0.032	8-10-14-18
3/4	0.032	6-8-10-14-18
1	0.035	6-8-10-14

radius than a wider blade. However, narrow width blades will break more easily when the feed rate is too great. The following shows the minimum radius that can usually be sawed with blades of various widths:

POWER SAWING	
Blade Width	Radius
1/2" (13 mm)	2 1/2" (64 mm)
3/8" (10 mm)	1 1/4" (32 mm)
1/4" (6 mm)	5/8" (16 mm)
3/16"(5 mm)	3/8"(10 mm)
1/8" (3 mm)	7/32" (6 mm)
3/32" (2 mm)	1/8" (3 mm)

Blade Thickness

Blades are available in the thicknesses shown in Fig. 4-9.

Teeth Per Inch

Teeth per inch refers to the **coarseness** of the teeth. It is also called **pitch**. Blades may have different degrees of coarseness, as shown in Fig. 4-9. A coarse pitch should be chosen for sawing large sections or thicknesses and soft metals. A finer pitch should be selected for sawing thinner thicknesses and harder metals. A minimum of two teeth should be in contact with the work at all times. The only exception is very thin sheet metal which is cut at higher speeds. For general metal cutting, band saw

blades of the following pitches will produce good results:

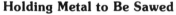

PITCHES	
Teeth Per Inch	Metal Thickness
18	up to 1/4 " (64 mm)
14	1/4 " to 1/2 " (6 to 13 mm)
10	1/2 " to 2 " (13 to 51 mm)
8	2" (51 mm) and larger

Skip-Tooth Blades

Some blades for metal-cutting band saws are of the skip-tooth type. They have a wide space between each tooth, as though every second tooth were removed. The wide space provides extra chip clearance. These may be used for sawing nonferrous metals, such as aluminum, brass, copper, lead, and zinc. Skip-tooth blades are also used to saw wood, plastic, asbestos, and other nonmetallic materials. They can be used at higher operating speeds than standard blades with regular teeth. This allows them to cut many times faster. Figure 4-10 shows speeds for general skip-tooth sawing.

Holding Metal to Be Sawed

To cut a piece of metal in the power hacksaw, clamp the stock to be cut tightly in the vise. See view **A** of Fig. 4-7. Suppose the bar from which a piece is to be cut is so short that it

Fig. 4-10
Cutting Speeds (sfpm) for
Skip-Tooth Band Saw Blades

Material	Speed in Feet Per Minute
Aluminum	2000 to 3000
Aluminum Alloys	300 to 2000
Asbestos	800 to 1500
Bakelite	2500 to 3500
Brass	400 to 1000
Copper	1000 to 1500
Formica	800 to 2000
Lucite-Plexiglas	2000 to 3000
Magnesium	3000 to 5000
Wood	2000 to 3000

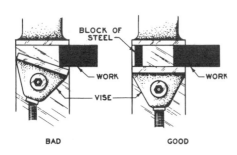

Fig. 4-11. Holding a short piece of metal in the power saw vise.

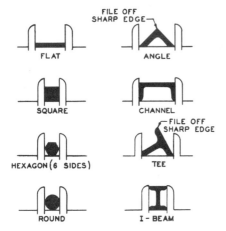

Fig. 4-12. Holding different shapes of metal in the power saw vise.

will not reach across the full width of the vise. Then you must put a piece of metal the same width as the bar at the other end of the vise. See Fig. 4-11. The pressure on both ends of the vise must be the same. Figure 4-12 shows how to hold various shapes of metal in the power saw vise. On some saws the vise may be swiveled up to 45° to make angular cuts.

One end of a long bar may be supported on a stock support. See Fig. 4-3. Both ends of the long bar should be the same height from the floor.

Measuring Metal to Be Cut

When you measure a piece of metal to be cut in the power hacksaw, place the edge of the rule alongside the metal to be cut. At the same

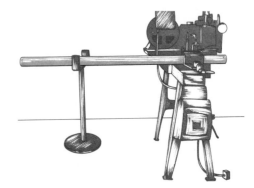

Fig. 4-13. Supporting a long piece of stock.

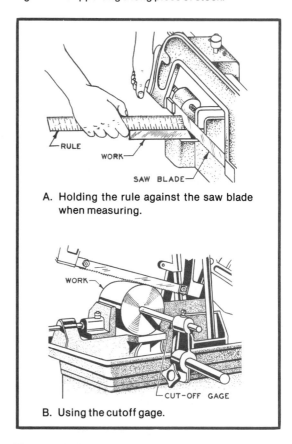

A. Holding the rule against the saw blade when measuring.

B. Using the cutoff gage.

Fig. 4-14. Measuring metal to be cut.

time, hold the end of the rule against the side of the saw blade, Fig. 4-14. While it is in this position, move the metal to the length wanted. Then tighten the vise against the metal.

CHISELS AND CHIPPING

Chipping is the art of shaping metal by removing small pieces with a cold chisel and a hammer. Most of the shaping that was once done by chipping is now done by machine tools. However, chipping is still done in maintenance and repair work.

Cold chisels are used to cut metal that has not been softened by heating. They are made of high-grade steel in a number of sizes and shapes. The cutting ends are hardened and tempered because the cutting tool must be harder than the material to be cut. The cutting angle is a wedge which cuts into the metal. See Fig. 4-15.

Cold chisels are known by the shapes of their cutting edges. They are called the flat chisel, cape chisel, diamond point chisel, and round nose chisel. See Fig. 4-16.

Holding Chisel and Hammer

Hold the middle of the chisel loosely in one hand. See view **A** of Fig. 4-17. For small, fine

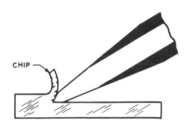

Fig. 4-15. Wedge action of a cold chisel.

A. Flat chisel — used for general cutting.

B. Cape chisel — used to cut narrow grooves.

C. Diamond chisel — used to cut V-shaped grooves.

D. Round nose chisel — used to chip around corners.

Fig. 4-16. Cold chisels.

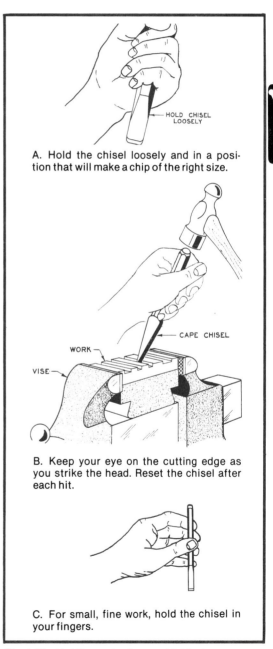

A. Hold the chisel loosely and in a position that will make a chip of the right size.

B. Keep your eye on the cutting edge as you strike the head. Reset the chisel after each hit.

C. For small, fine work, hold the chisel in your fingers.

Fig. 4-17. Holding and using a cold chisel.

Fig. 4-18. Always wear safety glasses or goggles when chipping.

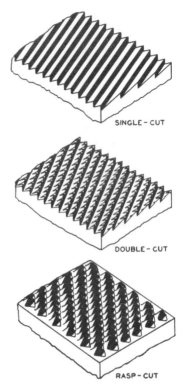

SINGLE - CUT

DOUBLE - CUT

RASP - CUT

Fig. 4-20. Cutting action of file.

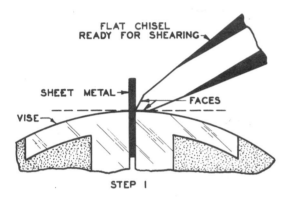

FLAT CHISEL READY FOR SHEARING

SHEET METAL

FACES

VISE

STEP I

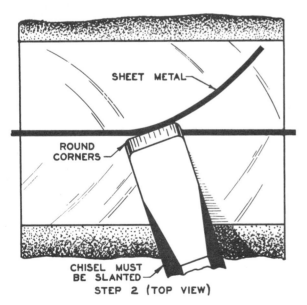

SHEET METAL

ROUND CORNERS

CHISEL MUST BE SLANTED

STEP 2 (TOP VIEW)

Fig. 4-19. Shearing sheet metal with a flat cold chisel.

work, hold it in the fingers, as shown in view **C**. Grasp the hammer handle near the end and hold it loosely to keep from tiring the arm. Always wear safety glasses, Fig. 4-18.

SHEARING

The vise jaw and flat chisel may be used together to act like a pair of scissors or shears. This is called **shearing.**

Thick sheet metal may be cut in a vise with a flat chisel. First, use your scriber to mark a guideline. Then, clamp the metal tightly in a vise that has good edges. The line should be just below the tops of the vise jaws. This leaves a little metal for filing to the line afterwards. Continue with these steps as shown in Fig. 4-19.

1. Lay the cutting edge of the chisel on top of the vise jaws and against the metal.

2. Slant the chisel a little. Make sure that the face of the chisel is horizontal as shown. This is important to making a square cut.
3. Start shearing cut.

FILES

Metal can be shaped with files of many shapes and sizes. However, only limited shaping is done with a file. Usually, the file is used to round corners, bevel edges, remove marks made by other tools, and for work where only a small amount of metal is cut away. The file cuts as it is moved in a forward stroke across the metal, Fig. 4-20.

Using a File

The file can cut all kinds of metal except hardened steel. Many files are dulled because the teeth touch the hardened jaws of a vise during the filing process. The file should be used only on metal which is **not as hard as the file** itself.

Use a file with a handle. Use only a file with sharp teeth. Grasp the handle of the file with your strong hand. Hold the palm against the end of the handle with the thumb on top, Fig. 4-21. Place the palm of the other hand on the point of the file with the fingers against the underside, as shown. For light filing, place the thumb of the left hand on the top of the file, Fig. 4-22.

Place the point of the file on the work. Cut by pressing down on the forward stroke, called the **cutting stroke.** Lift a little on the return stroke to prevent dulling the file. The file cuts only on the **cutting stroke.** Keep the file level on the work. Otherwise, the filed surface will be rounded and uneven instead of flat. Use the full length of the file and use smooth strokes. This is called **cross-filing.**

Cleaning a File

File teeth often become clogged with chips and filings called **pins.** These small chips stick in the teeth and scratch the work. Keep

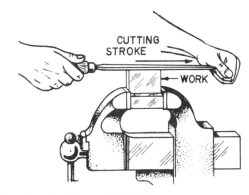
Fig. 4-21. Holding the file for filing.

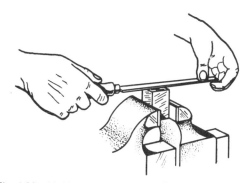
Fig. 4-22. Holding the file for light filing.

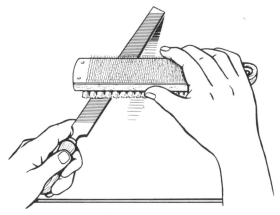
Fig. 4-23. Cleaning a file with file card and brush.

the file free from chips and filings. Brush it with a wire brush called a **file card,** Fig. 4-23.

Rub the file card over the file in the direction of the cuts. Sometimes the pins stick so tightly that the file card will not remove them.

Fig. 4-24
Files and Their Uses

Name and Shape of File	Kind of Cut	Uses
 WARDING FILE, parallel faces, edges taper to the point. Very thin.	Double-cut	Filing notches as in keys. Much used by **locksmiths.** Gets name from **ward,** meaning a notch in a key.
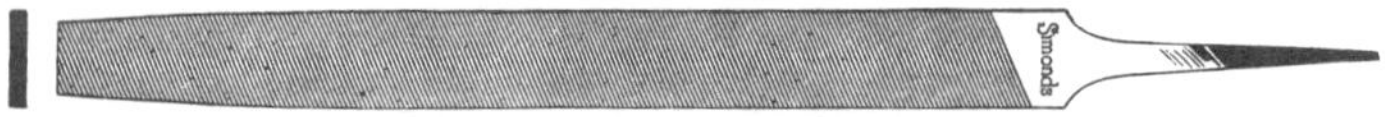 MILL FILE, tapered or blunt.	Single-cut	**Drawfiling,** finishing, and lathe work. Also used for finishing brass and bronze.
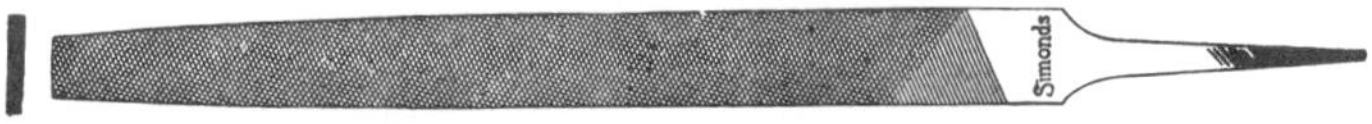 FLAT FILE, tapered in width and thickness.	Double-cut	One of the most commonly used files for general work.
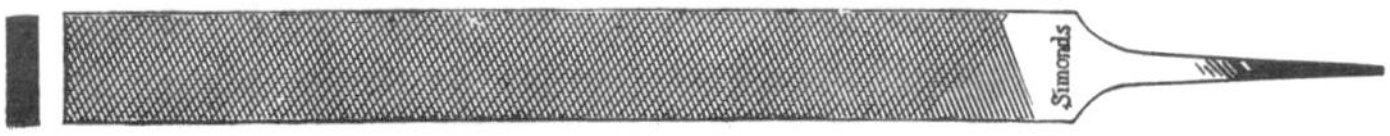 HAND FILE, equal in width and tapered in thickness, one safe edge.	Double-cut	Finishing flat surfaces. Has one **safe edge** and, therefore, is useful where the flat file cannot be used.
 PILLAR FILE, equal in width and tapered in thickness. One safe edge. Narrower and thicker than hand file.	Double-cut	Used for narrow work, such as **keyways** (see § 26-26), slots, and grooves.
 SQUARE FILE, tapered or blunt.	Double-cut	Filing square corners. Enlarging square or **rectangular**[1] openings as **splines**[2] and **keyways.**
 ROUND FILE (rat-tail), tapered.	Single-cut or Double-cut	Filing curved surfaces and enlarging round holes and forming **fillets.**[3]
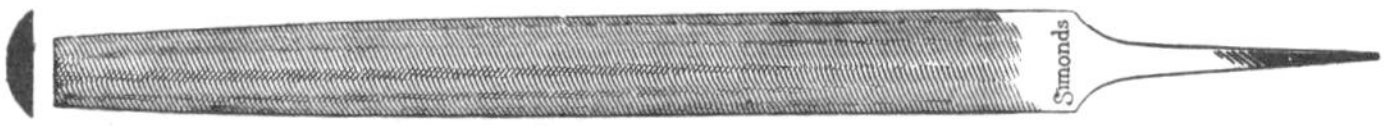 HALF-ROUND FILE, tapered. Not a half circle; only about one-third of a circle.	Double-cut	Filing curved surfaces.
 THREE-SQUARE FILE, tapered.	Double-cut	Filing corners and angles less than 90°, such as on **taps, cutters,**[4] etc., before they are hardened.
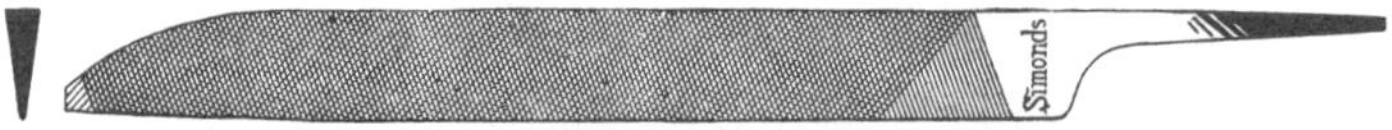 KNIFE FILE, tapered in width and thickness, shaped like a knife.	Double-cut	Filing narrow slots, notches, and grooves.

[1]Rectangular means having four 90° angles.

[2]A spline is a long feather key fastened to a shaft so that the pulley or gear may slide along the shaft lengthwise, both turning together.

[3]A fillet is a curve that fills the angle made by two connecting surfaces to avoid a sharp angle.

[4]A cutter is a sharp tool fixed in a machine for cutting metal.

DRILLING

Using a drill to cut a hole is called **drilling.** This process involves a drill and a tool for holding the drill.

The **hand drill** is a common holding tool for drilling holes in thin metal. See view **A** of Fig. 4-25. A small machine that can be carried easily from place to place is the **portable electric drill,** view **B.** The size of the tool refers to the maximum size of drill that will fit into the chuck or holder. A ½ " portable electric drill holds a ½ " drill. (It is important that portable electric tools are grounded to prevent electrical shock.)

Small, light work may be drilled on the handfeed drill press. Only the smaller drills are used on this press. The drill may be one that sets on the bench, called a bench drill. Or, it may be a floor model, as shown in view **C** of Fig. 4-25. It is the simplest drill press. It may seem sensitive because you can feel all the strains on the drill in the feed handle.

Drilling Speed and Feed

Drilling **speed** refers to the speed the drill turns or to the number of revolutions per minute. The **feed** is the distance the drill cuts into the metal during one turn or revolution. Both the speed and feed that are correct for a given drilling job depend on several things:

1. The diameter of hole to be drilled,
2. The material from which the drill is made, and
3. The hardness of the metal.

A general rule to follow is the smaller the diameter of the drill, the greater the speed should be. Likewise, the larger the diameter, the slower the speed should be. Also, hard metals require slower drill speed than soft metals. The pressure or force on the drill should be enough to keep it cutting. If the drill is allowed to turn without cutting, the drill will get hot and wear out quickly.

Drills are made of carbon steel, high-speed steel, and tungsten carbide. If the drill shank is not stamped HS, meaning high speed, it is made of carbon steel. High-speed steel drills cost two or three times as much as carbon-steel

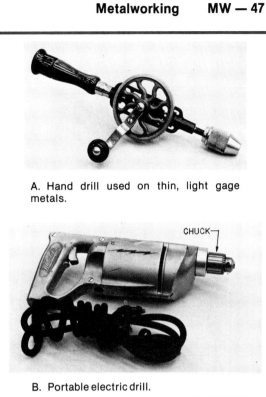

A. Hand drill used on thin, light gage metals.

B. Portable electric drill.

The Clausing Corp.

C. Hand feed floor drill press.

Fig. 4-25. Types of drilling machines.

drills. For drilling very hard or very abrasive materials, either tungsten carbide-tipped or solid tungsten carbide drills are available.

Sizes of Drills

Small drills are usually purchased in sets. The size of a drill is known by its diameter. The diameter may be a number gage, a letter, or a fractional size. Figure 4-26 shows the sizes from the smallest twist drill (No. 80) up to 1" in diameter.

Gage Numbers

Number drills are made in sizes from No. 80 to No. 1 (0.0135" to 0.228" diameters). Note that the larger the number, the smaller the drill.

ABRASIVES

Abrasive comes from the word **abrade,** which means to rub off. An abrasive substance is a very hard, tough material. It has many sharp cutting edges and points when crushed and ground into grains like sand. Abrasives must be

Fig. 4-26
Drill Sizes

Number and Letter Drills	Fractional Drills	Decimal Equivalents	Number and Letter Drills	Fractional Drills	Decimal Equivalents	Number and Letter Drills	Fractional Drills	Decimal Equivalents	Number and Letter Drills	Fractional Drills	Decimal Equivalents
80	...	.0135	42	...	.0935		13/64	.2031		13/32	.4062
79	...	.0145		3/32	.0937	6	...	.2040	Z	...	.4130
	1/64	.0156	41	...	.0960	5	...	.2055		27/64	.4219
78	...	.0160	40	...	.0980	4	...	.2090		7/16	.4375
77	...	.0180	39	...	.0995	3	...	.2130		29/64	.4531
76	...	.0200	38	...	.1015		7/32	.2187		15/32	.4687
75	...	.0210	37	...	.1040	2	...	.2210		31/64	.4844
74	...	.0225	36	...	.1065	1	...	.2280		1/2	.5000
73	...	.0240		7/64	.1094	A	...	.2340			
72	...	.0250	35	...	.1100		15/64	.2344		33/64	.5156
71	...	.0260	34	...	.1110	B	...	.2380		17/32	.5312
70	...	.0280	33	...	.1130	C	...	.2420		35/64	.5469
69	...	.0292	32	...	.1160	D	...	.2460		9/16	.5625
68	...	.0310	31*	...	.1200	E	1/4	.2500		37/64	.5781
	1/32	.0312		1/8	.1250	F	...	.2570		19/32	.5937
67	...	.0320	30	...	.1285	G	...	.2610		39/64	.6094
66	...	.0330	29	...	.1360		17/64	.2656		5/8	.6250
65	...	.0350	28	...	.1405	H	...	.2660			
64	...	.0360		9/64	.1406	I	...	.2720		41/64	.6406
63	...	.0370	27	...	.1440	J	...	.2770		21/32	.6562
62	...	.0380	26	...	.1470	K	...	.2810		43/64	.6719
61	...	.0390	25	...	.1495		9/32	.2812		11/16	.6875
60	...	.0400	24	...	.1520	L	...	.2900		45/64	.7031
59	...	.0410	23	...	.1540	M	...	.2950		23/32	.7187
58	...	.0420		5/32	.1562		19/64	.2969		47/64	.7344
57	...	.0430	22	...	.1570	N	...	.3020		3/4	.7500
56	...	.0465	21	...	.1590		5/16	.3125			
	3/64	.0469	20	...	.1610	O	...	.3160		49/64	.7656
55	...	.0520	19	...	.1660	P	...	.3230		25/32	.7812
54	...	.0550	18	...	.1695		21/64	.3281		51/64	.7969
53	...	.0595		11/64	.1719	Q	...	.3320		13/16	.8125
	1/16	.0625	17	...	.1720	R	...	.3390		53/64	.8281
52	...	.0635	16	...	.1770		11/32	.3437		27/32	.8437
51	...	.0670	15	...	.1800	S	...	.3480		55/64	.8594
50	...	.0700	14	...	.1820	T	...	.3580		7/8	.8750
49	...	.0730	13	...	.1850		23/64	.3594		57/64	.8906
48	...	.0760		3/16	.1875	U	...	.3680		29/32	.9062
	5/64	.0781	12	...	.1890		3/8	.3750		59/64	.9219
47	...	.0785	11	...	.1910	V	...	.3770		15/16	.9375
46	...	.0810	10	...	.1935	W	...	.3860		61/64	.9531
45	...	.0820	9	...	.1960		25/64	.3906		31/32	.9687
44	...	.0860	8	...	.1990	X	...	.3970		63/64	.9844
43	...	.0890	7	...	.2010	Y	...	.4040		1	1.0000

harder than the materials they cut. Several common forms in which abrasives are used in metalworking include:

1. Abrasive cloth (also called coated abrasive).
2. Loose grain and powder abrasive.
3. Abrasive compounds (in the form of paste, sticks, or cakes).
4. Grinding wheels.
5. Sharpening stones.

Abrasives are used for (1) sharpening, (2) polishing, and (3) removing material.

Kinds of Abrasives

The common abrasive materials are classed as either natural or artificial. See Fig. 4-27. **Natural abrasives** are minerals. They occur either in the form of grains, like sand, or in the form of large rocklike chunks. The large chunks must be crushed or ground into small abrasive grains. Some common natural abrasives include flint, garnet, emery, corundum, crocus, and diamond.

The **artificial abrasives** are also known as synthetic or manufactured abrasives. With the exception of diamond, artificial abrasives are harder than the natural abrasives. Diamond is the hardest abrasive material. Artificial abrasives have largely replaced the natural abrasives in metalworking because of their hardness and wear resistance.

POLISHING

Coated abrasives, powdered abrasives, and abrasive compounds are used to remove small amounts of metal. This is frequently done as a final operation to improve the surface appearance. In this **polishing process,** the surface scratches made by the abrasive particles get smaller as smaller size abrasives are used. All scratches must be in the same direction since light reflection affects the appearance. Abrasives are also used to remove small amounts of metal. This would be to improve the way parts fit together. Sometimes polishing is done by applying an abrasive compound on a revolving cloth wheel. In this case, you must be careful to keep hair and clothing away from the wheel.

The Norton Company

Fig. 4-27. Some commonly used coated abrasives.

GRINDING AND SHARPENING

Grinding is a machining process. Metal is removed from the workpiece either with a revolving abrasive (grinding) wheel, a moving abrasive belt, a disc, or some other form. When the workpiece is brought into contact with the abrasive tool, tiny chips of metal are removed. See Fig. 4-28. Because of frictional heat, the chips may appear as red-hot sparks right after leaving the workpiece. They are rapidly cooled by air. Abrasive tools remove metal in chip form in much the same way as do lathe tools, saw blades, and milling cutters.

The term **grinding** is used when a small amount of metal is removed. This might be in tool sharpening and in finishing hardened steel workpieces to size. **Abrasive machining** is the use of abrasive tools to remove large amounts of metal quickly in order to produce a workpiece of desired shape and size.

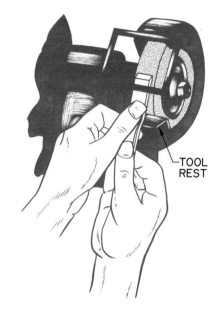

Fig. 4-28. Sharpening a cold chisel on a grinding wheel.

Safety Note

In any operation involving abrasives, safety glasses or goggles should be worn. When revolving wheels are used in the **abrading** processes, be sure that your hair and clothing are kept away from moving parts.

Chapter **5**

FORGING AND FORMING

Metalworking processes that shape metal without removing material are called forming processes.

FORGING

Forging is a type of forming. It is the oldest of the metalworking processes. The process consists of hammering or pressing the metal into the desired shape. This may be done with or without the use of **dies** which give shape or form to metal. Forging may be done hot or cold, but is usually understood to mean hot forging. Almost all forged parts are now produced with machines. Hand forging is limited largely to repair work and making custom parts.

Advantages and Disadvantages

When metal is hot, it is in a soft, plastic (pliable) state. It is easily formed under pressure without breaking. Other advantages include these:

1. Forged parts are stronger than machined parts of the same material. **Machining** cuts through the grain. **Forging** causes the grain to follow the shape of the workpiece, Fig. 5-1. Metal is **strongest in the direction of grain flow.**
2. Strong parts of complex shape can be produced at less cost than by machining.
3. Since shape is produced by hammering, not cutting, much less metal is lost in the process.

There are several disadvantages:

1. The high forging temperatures cause rapid oxidation. This causes a surface scale to form which results in a poor finish.
2. Because of scaling, close tolerances cannot be obtained.
3. Care must be taken to prevent contact with the metal and to avoid flying scale.

HAND FORGING

Hand forging is now done mostly by service workers who maintain production equipment, tools, and machines. Sometimes the workers construct product pilot models or prototypes by hand forging.

Equipment for Hand Forging

Metal to be forged is usually heated either in a gas furnace or in a gas forge. Care must be taken when lighting this equipment. Automatic

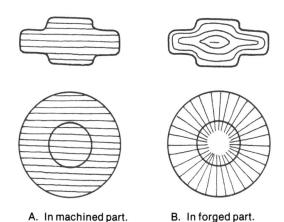

A. In machined part.   B. In forged part.

Fig. 5-1.   Comparison of grain patterns.

lighting systems with electrical ignition are safest.

Lighting procedure generally calls for the following steps:

1. Switch on the blower motor, but keep the air valve **closed.**
2. Open the gas valve part way.
3. Immediately ignite the gas either electrically or with a torch. The torch can be made of a rolled up paper towel placed in the combustion chamber.
4. Open the air and gas valves as far as needed to get a clean-burning flame of the desired size.

--- Safety Note ---
Never let gas accumulate in a furnace chamber before it is ignited. An explosion will result.

5. When turning the forge off, always **shut off the gas first** and then the air.

In hand forging, metal is hammered to shape on an **anvil,** Fig. 5-2. The anvil body is made of soft steel. The face is made of hardened steel and welded to the body.

The **horn** is shaped like a cone. It is tough and unhardened. Rings, hooks, and other curved parts are formed on it.

The **cutting block** is located between the face and the horn. Its surface is not hardened. Metal may be cut or chipped upon it with a cold chisel. The face of the anvil should not be used for chipping.

The **hardy hole** is a square hole in the face of the anvil. Various tools are held in the hole for different kinds of work.

The **pritchel hole** is the small, round hole in the face of the anvil. It is used to bend small rods and punch holes in metal.

Anvils weigh from a few pounds (kilograms) to as much as 300 pounds (136 kilograms). One weighing between 100 and 200 pounds (45 and 90 kilograms) is suitable for school use. It should be fastened securely to a stable wood or metal base which will position the face of the anvil about 30″ (0.8 m) from the floor.

Tongs are used to hold and handle the hot metal, Fig. 5-3. Some of the types of tongs are listed below:

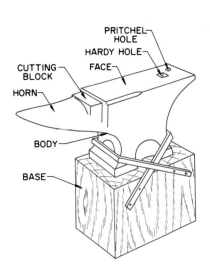

Fig. 5-2.   Anvil.

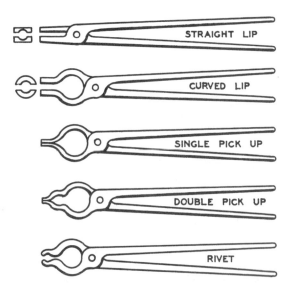

Fig. 5-3.   Tongs.

Fig. 5-4.   Holding work with tongs.

1. Straight-lip tong, also called flat-jawed tong — used to hold flat work.
2. Curved-lip tong, sometimes called bolt tong — used to hold round work, such as bolts or rivets. The opening behind the jaws allows space for the head of a bolt.
3. Single pickup tong — used to pick up either flat work or round work.
4. Double pickup tong — used to pick up either flat work or round work.
5. Rivet tong — used to hold square or round work, such as rivets or bolts.

Always use tongs that will grip the work firmly, Fig. 5-4. A ring, or link, may be slipped over the handles to hold them together. It holds the work firmly and relieves the hand of the strain. The job is slowed up if the tongs do not fit the work. There is also danger of the hot work slipping out of the tongs. Workers could be injured. Never leave the tongs in the fire with the work.

Hammers and sledges with many types of heads are used in hand forging. The hammers used for light forge work are shown in Fig. 5-5. One is the blacksmith hand hammer. The other is a sledge. It is a large, heavy hammer with a long handle. It is swung with both hands. Sledges weigh from 8 to 20 pounds (3.6 to 9 kilograms).

The set hammer has a smooth, flat face about 1¼ " (32 mm) square, Fig. 5-6. It is used to make square corners and shoulders. It is placed on the work and then the other end is struck with a hammer or sledge.

The **flatter** has a flat, smooth face about 2½ " (64 mm) square with rounded edges. See Fig. 5-6. It is used for the same kind of work as the set hammer except that the flatter has a larger face.

The **hardy** is a tool similar to a chisel, Figs. 5-7 and 5-8. It has a square shank and is used to

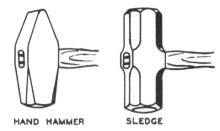

Fig. 5-5.   Blacksmith hand hammer and sledge.

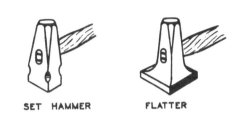

Fig. 5-6.   Set hammer and flatter.

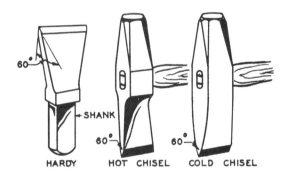

Fig. 5-7.   Hardy and blacksmith chisels.

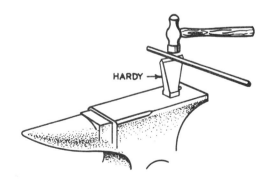

Fig. 5-8.   Cutting metal with a hardy.

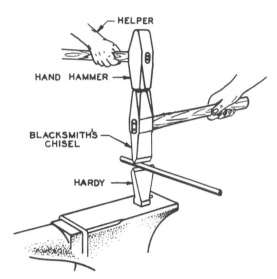

Fig. 5-9.   Cutting metal with a blacksmith chisel and hardy.

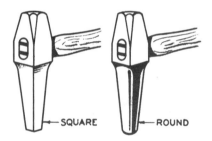

Fig. 5-10.   Blacksmith punches.

Fig. 5-11.   Punching.

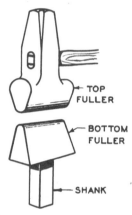

Fig. 5-12.   Fullers.

cut hot and cold metal. The square shank is placed in the hardy hole of the anvil. The metal to be cut is then laid on the cutting edge and struck with a hammer.

Blacksmith chisels, often called cutters, are fitted with handles. There are two kinds. One is used to cut cold metal and is called a cold chisel or cold cutter. The other is used to cut hot metal and is called a hot chisel or hot cutter. Note in Fig. 5-7 that the one used to cut hot metal is much thinner than the one used to cut cold metal. One should not be used in place of the other. Both sides of the metal should be cut or nicked only part way through with a blacksmith chisel and hardy, Fig. 5-9, and then

broken. Thin metal may be cut on the cutting block of the anvil. See Fig. 5-2.

Blacksmith punches, Fig. 5-10, are used to punch holes in hot metal. They are made in different sizes and shapes. The punches are tapered.

To use a punch, heat the metal to a bright red color. Lay it flat on the anvil. Place the punch on the spot where the hole is to be made. Strike a heavy blow with the hammer. Keep striking the punch until it goes into the metal with difficulty, Fig. 5-11. Quickly remove the punch and cool it. Turn the metal over. Lay it so that the punched part will be exactly over the pritchel hole. See Fig. 5-2. Place the punch on the bulge made by punching from the other side and drive it through.

Forming tools of different shapes, used to make grooves or hollows, are called **fullers**, Fig. 5-12. They are often used in pairs. The bottom

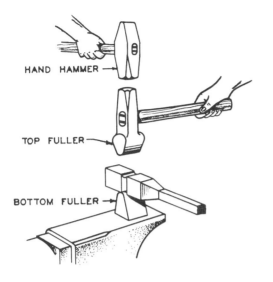

Fig. 5-13. Fullering with top and bottom fullers.

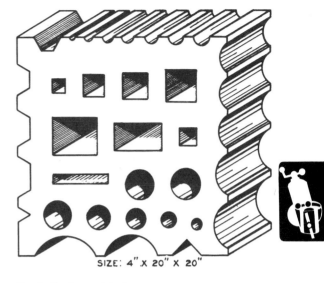

SIZE: 4" X 20" X 20"

Fig. 5-15. Swage block.

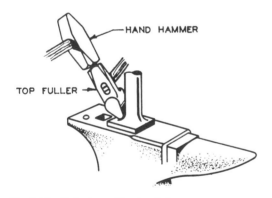

Fig. 5-14. Fullering with a top fuller.

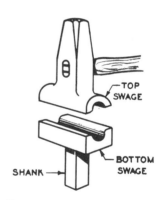

Fig. 5-16. Swages.

fuller has a square shank that fits into the hardy hole in the anvil. The top fuller has a handle.

Fullering is the using of fullers. The work is placed on the bottom fuller. Then the top fuller is placed on the work and struck with a hammer, Fig. 5-13. The top fuller is also used as in Fig. 5-14. It is used to stretch or spread metal the same as when peening with a cross peen or straight peen hammer.

A **swage block,** Fig. 5-15, is a heavy block of cast iron or steel about 4" (102 mm) thick and

from 16" to 20" (406 to 508 mm) square. It has many different grooves and holes. These are used to form metal into different shapes. The swage block can be set up in any position and often takes the place of bottom swages.

Swages are grooved tools used to smooth or finish round bars or surfaces. Fig. 15-16. They are often used in pairs. The bottom swage fits into the hardy hole in the anvil. The work is laid in the groove of the bottom swage. The top swage has a handle. It is placed over the work and struck with a hammer, making a smooth, round surface. Each swage is made for a round bar of a certain size. Swages are also made for other shapes.

FORMING MILD STEEL

Soft steel is formed to produce ornamental and useful designs. The steel is bent, twisted, beat, peened, or hammered.

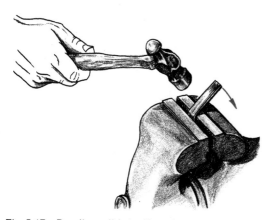

Fig. 5-17.   Bending mild steel in a vise.

Bending

Bending may be done by holding the metal in a vise and striking it with a hammer, Fig. 5-17. It may be bent around other objects such as a pipe, Fig. 5-18, or formed with **bending jigs,** Fig. 5-19.

Simple forming, such as bending band iron to a right angle, is done by holding the metal securely between the jaws of a machinist's vise. It is then pounded into shape with repeated blows of a hammer. Very heavy material must be heated and worked while it is red hot. Other forming may be done by holding the metal on the horn of an anvil or some other object as it is hammered into shape.

Bending jigs are used to make decorative scrolls and other shapes often used in ornamental ironwork. When several pieces of the same shape are needed, permanent bending jigs may be made from wood or metal to form the metal. These jigs are useful when turning out items in mass production. Some of these jigs are simple enough that they can be easily made in the average shop. Others are very complicated and are often operated by machines.

A variety of forms may be produced by using the jig shown in Fig. 5-20. Scrolls or other complicated shapes are gradually formed to the desired shape by changing the position of the metal in the jig.

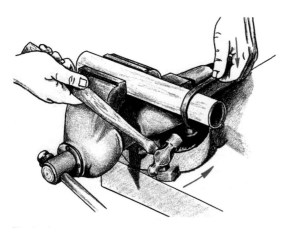

Fig. 5-18.   Bending mild steel around a pipe.

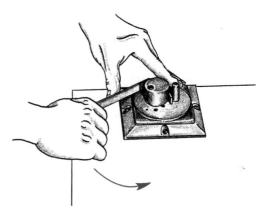

Fig. 5-19.   Forming metal with a bending jig.

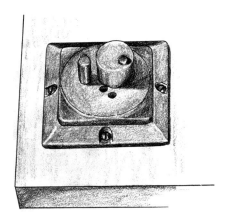

Fig. 5-20. Bending jig.

Fig. 5-21. Peening metal.

HAMMERING AND PEENING

Hammering

Mild steel is malleable. That is, it can be shaped by hammering. This allows mild steel to be worked while it is hot or cold. When much forming is to be done, the metal should be heated and pounded out while it is red hot. However, most forming of ornamental ironwork can be done while the metal is cold.

Peening

Peening is an effective way to decorate the surface of mild steel. Hit the metal with uniform blows of a ball peen hammer to cover the area with small overlapping indentations. See Fig. 5-21. This produces an antique appearance which resembles hand wrought iron.

Twisting

A machinist's vise and a wrench are the only tools needed to twist sections of band iron or square stock.

1. Mark the metal at each end of the section to be twisted.
2. Hold one end of the metal in a vise with the vise jaws clamped at one of the marks.
3. Place the wrench at the other mark, Fig. 5-22.
4. Turn the wrench with a circular motion to twist the metal, Fig. 5-23. If identical parts

Fig. 5-22. Place wrench at top mark.

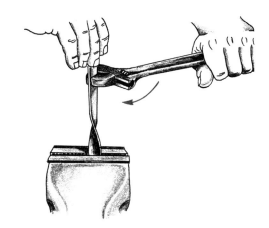

Fig. 5-23. Twisting metal.

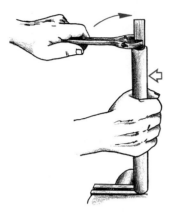

Fig. 5-24. Using pipe to support a long twisted section.

are to be made, the spacing between marks must be the same. The wrench must be turned the same number of times.

5. Support long sections as they are twisted to keep them from bowing. This can be done by slipping a pipe over the metal, Fig. 5-24.

FASTENING MILD STEEL

In most metalwork, pieces must be secured together in some way to hold them in place. Mild steel may be fastened with mechanical fasteners or by welding (Chapter 9).

Chapter **6**

SHEET METAL WORK

Metal sheets less than ¼" thick (.250" or 6.350 mm) are called sheet metal. Thickness is designated by gage numbers or by decimal parts of an inch. Metal sheet ¼" (6.350 mm) and more in thickness is termed **plate.** Its thickness is given in fractional parts of an inch or millimeters.

Sheet metal is used in many ways. It is often used in place of wood. Objects of sheet metal can be found everywhere. They include street and road signs, tool parts, toys, desks, and mailboxes. Washing and drying machine cabinets, television and file cabinets are also common sheet metal products. The sheet metals most used are steel, galvanized steel, tinplated steel, stainless steel, aluminum, copper, and brass.

Sheet metal thicknesses and wire diameters are specified either by gage numbers or by decimal fractions of an inch. Sheet metal and wire gages have slots which match the different gage sizes. See Fig. 6-1. The gage number is stamped on one side of the gage. The decimal equivalent of the gage number is stamped on the other.

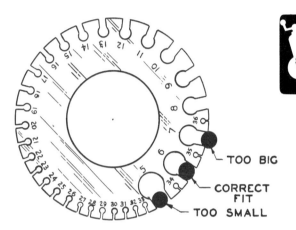

Fig. 6-1.   Sheet metal and wire gage.

SHEET METAL LAYOUT

Many things — cloth shirts, leather pocketbooks, plastic lampshades, and metal wastebaskets — are cut from sheet materials. They all require the use of a **pattern.** The pattern is made to the exact size and shape of the flat sheet material needed to form the object. A pattern is often called a **stretchout,** because it shows what the object looks like when

stretched flat. A metal pattern is called a **template** or **templet.**

The pattern for a box, for example, may be a flat piece of paper or cardboard. It is cut to the outline of the unfolded shape of the box, Fig. 6-2. Note how bending lines are shown. A small freehand circle is drawn at each end of the line.

The marking of lines on sheet metal is called **laying out.** There are three ways to lay out lines on sheet metal:

1. By drawing lines on paper and then transferring them to the sheet metal by using carbon paper.
2. By drawing lines on paper as before, then taping the paper to the sheet metal. This will keep it from slipping while you make small prick punch marks through the paper. Make punchmarks at all corners, intersections of lines, end of lines, and centers of arcs and circles. Curves are made by putting the

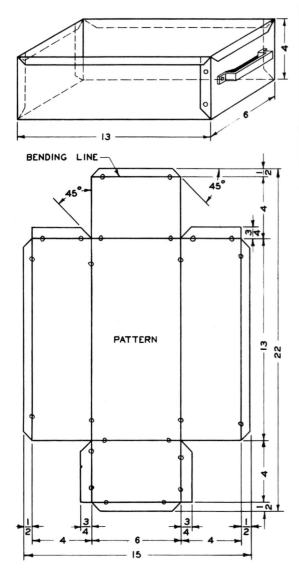

Fig. 6-2. Pattern for metal box.

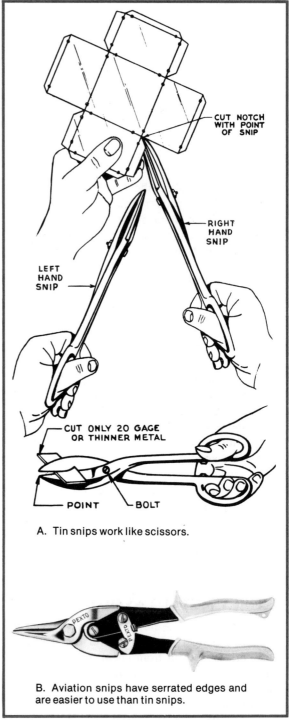

A. Tin snips work like scissors.

B. Aviation snips have serrated edges and are easier to use than tin snips.

Fig. 6-3. Using tin snips.

punch marks close together. After punching, the paper is removed. The punch marks are used as guides for scribing the lines, circles, and curves. Use a steel rule or square and a scriber or scratch awl to scribe the straight lines. Use a divider to make the circles and arcs.

3. By measuring and scribing the lines, directly on the sheet metal. If two or more pieces are to be cut alike, use the first piece of metal that has been cut as the template for the others.

CUTTING SHEET METAL

Many tools are available for cutting sheet metal. There are tin snips and aviation snips, Fig. 6-3. There are double-cutting shears, bench shears, squaring shears, notcher, ring and circle shears, and lever shears. Nibblers and portable electric shears are also used to cut thin-gage sheet metal.

Squaring Shear

The squaring shear, Fig. 6-4, is used to cut metal no thicker than 16-gage mild steel. It is operated by foot. It is handy for cutting strips of sheet metal and for cutting and trimming the edges square to each other. It should never be used for cutting wire or nails. This would cause the blade to be nicked and ruin it for use with sheet metal.

The side guides on the table help to keep the metal square with the cutting blades. The squaring shear cuts many pieces of the same size because the back gage can be locked at any desired setting. The fingers should be kept away from the blade, which should be guarded. The treadle should be fitted with a stop to prevent it from going all the way to the floor. This could injure the operator's foot.

DRILLING HOLES

Small holes, such as for rivets, sheet metal screws may be drilled with a drill press, portable electric drill, or hand drill. It is best to clamp the workpiece to the drill press table.
1. Mark the location of the hole.
2. Make a small indentation at the hole location with a center punch.
3. Place a hardwood board on the drill press table. Lay the sheet metal on top of it.
4. Align the drill with the hole location. Then secure the metal and board to the table with C clamps, Fig. 6-5.
5. Turn the drill press on. Then feed the drill slowly but steadily through the metal.

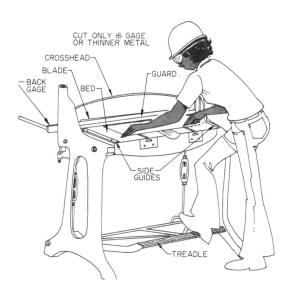

Fig. 6-4.   Squaring shear.

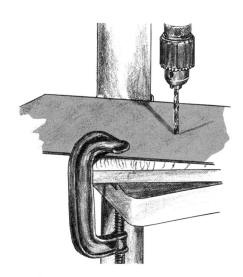

Fig. 6-5.   Clamp metal and board to the table.

PUNCHES

Hand punches, Fig. 6-6, may be used to punch holes in sheet metal. The hollow punch, Fig. 6-7, makes large holes to allow passage of bolts, cables, and pipes. The other punches make small holes for rivets, nails, and screws.

To use the solid punch or hollow punch, lay the metal on a block of lead or the end grain of hard wood. Place the punch on the sheet metal and strike with a hammer, Fig. 6-8.

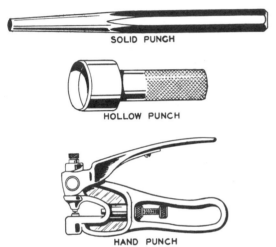

SOLID PUNCH

HOLLOW PUNCH

HAND PUNCH

Fig. 6-6.   Types of punches.

Fig. 6-7.   Driving the hollow punch through metal.

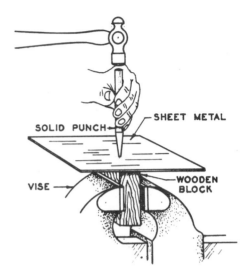

Fig. 6-8.   Punching a hole in sheet metal with a solid punch.

The hand punch is used as you would use a paper punch. It can be used only to punch holes near the edge of the metal.

BENDING

Making 90° Bends in Sheet Metal

Sheet metal is often formed to box-like shapes. Corners are notched and then bent up the sides at 90° to the bottom. This and similar operations are best done with a box and pan brake, as shown in Fig. 6-21. If the shop is not equipped with a pan brake, this operation can be done in a vise with hardwood blocks, Fig. 6-9.

1. Lay out the pattern and cut the metal to shape. Scribe a line to mark the location of each bend.
2. Clamp a hardwood board to the table with C clamps. Leave one edge extending out from the table slightly.
3. Cut two hardwood blocks. One block is made to fit the inside length of the box. The other is to fit the inside width of the box.
4. Lay the sheet metal on top of the long board. The location of the bend should line up with the edge of the board.

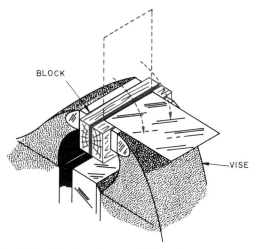

Fig. 6-9.   Bending sheet metal in a vise.

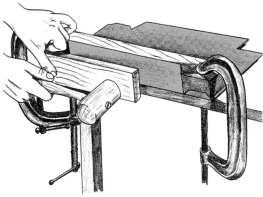

Fig. 6-11.   Making the fold with mallet and board.

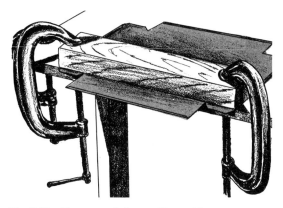

Fig. 6-10.   Sheet metal clamped in position.

5. Select the block which corresponds to the length of the side being formed. Place the block on top of the metal with its edge aligned with the location of the bend.
6. Secure the blocks and sheet metal with C clamps, Fig. 6-10.
7. Using a mallet, gradually tap the metal up against the top board to form the side. Another board may be held against the metal and hit with a mallet to aid in forming the side. See Fig. 6-11.
8. Bend the other sides up in the same way. Secure the metal with the board corresponding to the length of the side being formed.

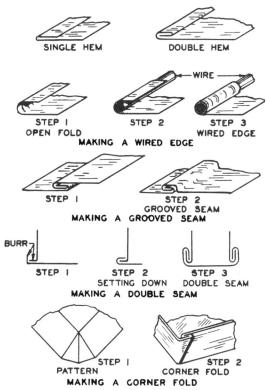

Fig. 6-12.   Hems and seams.

HEMS AND SEAMS

Several kinds of hems and seams are shown in Fig. 6-12. A **hem** is an edge or border made by folding. It stiffens the sheet of metal and folds the sharp edge inside. A **seam** is a joint made by fastening two edges together.

The single hem is normally made in the bar folder, Fig. 6-13. If a bar folder is not available, small pieces may be pinched and bent in a vise and then finished with a mallet. Large pieces can be hemmed in the following manner:

1. Scribe a line to locate the position of the fold to be made in forming the hem. Most hems are from ¼ " to ½ " (6 to 12 mm) wide.
2. Secure a hardwood board to the table with C clamps. Let one edge extend out from the table slightly, as shown in **A** of Fig. 6-14.
3. Lay the sheet metal on top of the board. Align the fold mark with the edge of the board.
4. Arrange another board on top of the metal with its edge lying along the scribed line which makes the fold.
5. Clamp the boards and metal to the table with C clamps, **B** of Fig. 6-14.
6. Bend the hem down gradually by tapping lightly with a wood or rubber mallet. Continue working back and forth along the metal until the hem is bent down against the bottom board, as in view **C**.
7. Lay the sheet metal flat on the table with the hem up.
8. Bend the hem over by working back and forth from one end to the other with light taps of the mallet. Continue until the hem is folded completely flat, **D** of Fig. 6-14.

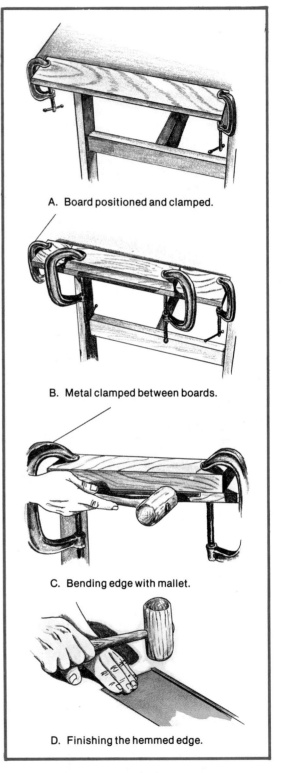

A. Board positioned and clamped.

B. Metal clamped between boards.

C. Bending edge with mallet.

D. Finishing the hemmed edge.

Fig. 6-13. Bar folder for making hems.

Fig. 6-14. Hemming a metal edge.

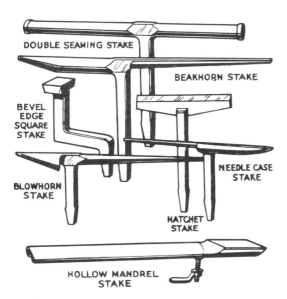

Fig. 6-15. Types of stakes.

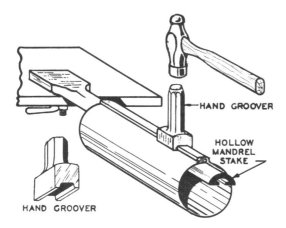

Fig. 6-16. A hand groover is used to groove and flatten a seam.

STAKES

Much of the forming in sheet metalwork must be done on stakes. See Fig. 6-15. The stake is supported by inserting the tapered square end in a matching hole in the bench plate.

The **double seaming stake** is used to make the double seam.

Fig. 6-17. Giant stamping (forming) press in an automobile plant.

The **beakhorn stake** is used to rivet, form round and square surfaces, bend straight edges, and make corners.

The **bevel-edged square stake** is used to form corners and edges.

The **hatchet stake** is used to make straight, sharp bends and to fold and bend edges.

Small tubes and pipes may be formed on the **needle-case stake.**

Cone-shaped articles may be formed on the **blowhorn stake.** The use of the hollow mandrel stake is shown in Fig. 6-16.

Sheet metal should be hammered with a mallet to keep from stretching and nicking it.

FORMING SHEET METAL WITH MOLDS

Most sheet metal is malleable and ductile enough that it can be pressed to the shape of a mold. The molds used in industry are made of metal and are called **dies.** Simple dies usually consist of two main parts. One part contains a cavity which has the same shape as the item to be formed. The other part of the die is made to fit inside the cavity in much the same way as a cake fits in a cake pan. These dies are mounted on machines which can force the two parts together under great pressure, Fig. 6-17. The sheet metal to be formed is placed between the two die parts. They are then forced together, pressing the sheet metal between them and forming it to shape.

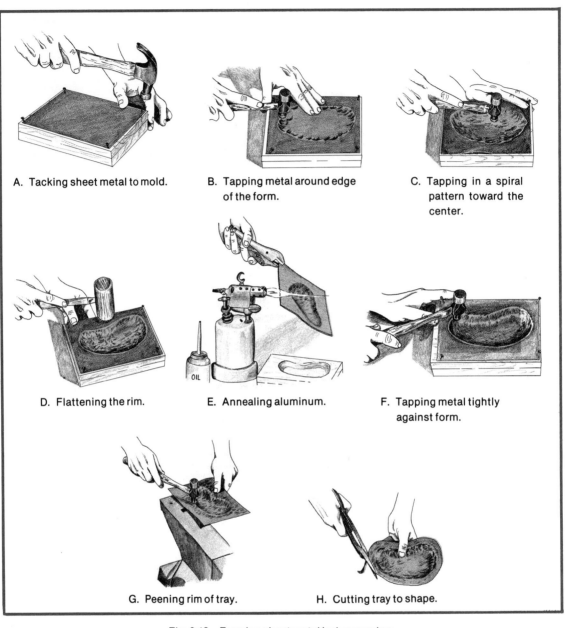

A. Tacking sheet metal to mold.

B. Tapping metal around edge of the form.

C. Tapping in a spiral pattern toward the center.

D. Flattening the rim.

E. Annealing aluminum.

F. Tapping metal tightly against form.

G. Peening rim of tray.

H. Cutting tray to shape.

Fig. 6-18. Forming sheet metal by hammering.

The forming of some items may require the use of more than one die. The sheet metal part is formed in several stages. Automobile body parts, housing for refrigerators, kitchen utensils, and many other items are formed by dies and power presses.

Simple projects, such as shallow bowls, ash trays, and candy dishes, can be formed by hammering sheet metal into a wood or metal mold. This method of forming takes much time and many taps with a hammer, but the principle is the same as that used in industry. Wood molds with circular cavities may be easily made on a wood turning lathe. Soft aluminum, brass, or copper can be readily stretched to conform to the shape of a mold.

1. Cut the sheet to size. The metal needed to make the depression will be about the size of the widest part plus the height and the width of the rim.

2. Hold the metal securely over the mold cavity. The edges of the metal may be taped to the mold with masking tape to help hold the sheet in place. If a waste rim (part of the metal which will later be trimmed off) is left, it may be clamped or nailed to the wood mold. See **A** of Fig. 6-18.

3. Tap the metal lightly around the edge of the cavity. The metal tapped down in this area will help keep the piece from slipping as you work, view **B**.

4. Continue tapping the metal with the peen end of the hammer in a spiral path toward the center, view **C**.

5. Flatten the rim occasionally to stretch it and prevent buckling, view **D**.

6. Aluminum, brass, and copper become hard and brittle when hammered. They must be softened at times if the depression is to be deeper than ¼ ″ (6 mm). Nonferrous metal may be annealed (softened) by heating, and then quenching in water. Copper and brass should be heated until they become red-hot before they are placed in water. Aluminum has a much lower melting point than copper or brass and cannot be heated to as high a temperature. Place oil on aluminum as a heat indicator when annealing. Heat the aluminum until the oil burns off. Then quench it in water. See view **E** of Fig. 6-18.

7. Continue tapping the metal from the outside edge of the cavity toward the center. It should be pressed against the bottom of the mold in all areas, as in view **F**.

8. Peen the rim of the tray by tapping it with the peen end of the hammer. Hit the metal with uniform blows of the hammer to form small overlapping depressions. At times it may be desirable to remove the tray from the mold and peen the rim on an anvil, as shown in view **G**.

9. Trim shape with tin snips, view **H**.

10. File the edges of the rim. Then smooth them with emery cloth.

11. Clean the object with steel wool.

FORMING BY MACHINE

The **grooving machine** grooves and flattens seams started on the bar folder. See Fig. 6-19.

The **bar folder** bends sheet metal edges to form seams and hems. See Fig. 6-20.

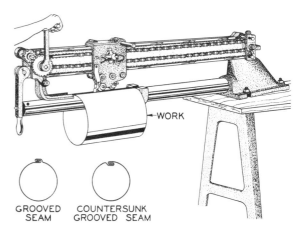

GROOVED SEAM   COUNTERSUNK GROOVED SEAM

Fig. 6-19. Grooving machine.

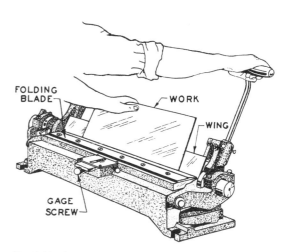

Fig. 6-20. The bar folder.

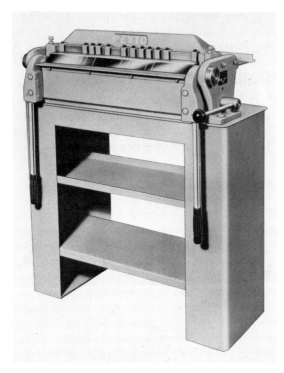

Fig. 6-21. Box and pan brake.

Combination Turning, Wiring, and Burring Machine

To make a rounded edge, set the gage about 2½ times the diameter of the wire away from the center of the groove in the roll. Be sure the rolls are set to fit each other. Then place the work on the lower roll and against the gage, Fig. 6-23. Screw down the top roll so that it grooves the work a little when turning the crank. Next, screw the upper roll down a little more, raise the work a little with the left hand, and turn the crank again. The groove is thus made deeper.

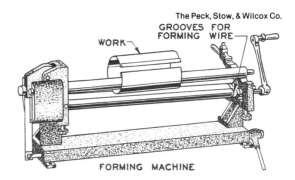

The Peck, Stow, & Wilcox Co.

The **box and pan brake** is designed to allow boxes, pans, or trays to be folded from one piece of metal. The upper jaw is made of a number of blocks of different widths. These blocks can be put together in any combination so as to make a bend of any width desired, Fig. 6-21.

The **slip-roll forming machine** forms stove pipes, cans, etc., out of flat sheet metal. See Fig. 6-22. The machine has three rolls which can be set different distances apart. The curves are formed between the rolls. If the metal to be formed has a wired edge, the wired edge may be slipped into one of the grooves at one end of the rolls.

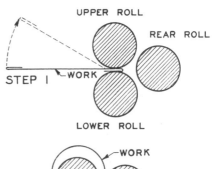

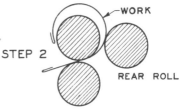

Fig. 6-22. Forming with rolls on the slip-roll forming machine.

Repeat these steps several times. Each time screw the top roll down a little more. Raise the work with the left hand until the work held with the left hand is straight up and down and touches the side of the top roll. The groove, or rounded edge, is now ready for the wire and may be taken out of the machine.

After the edge of the work has been made round in the turning machine, the wire is placed into the rounded edge. The edge is hammered over a little with a mallet. The metal edge may then be completely pressed over the wire with a wiring machine, Fig. 6-24. The wired edge may be used on flat work as well as round work.

The burring machine, Fig. 6-25 is used to make a burr on the edge of the bottom for a can and on the end of a cylinder. The handling of the metal with the left hand is the same as when turning the edge on the turning machine.

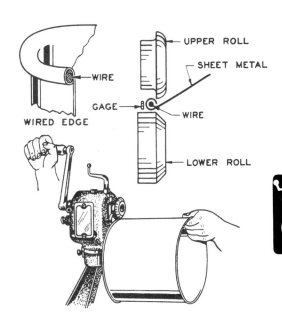

Fig. 6-24. Wiring an edge.

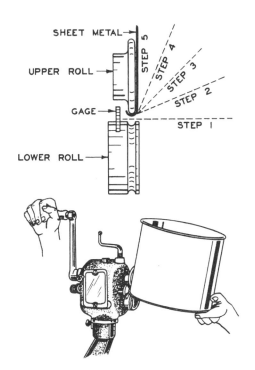

Fig. 6-23. Turning an edge.

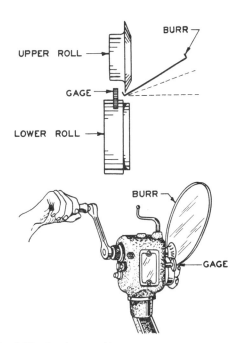

Fig. 6-25. Burring machine.

ART METALWORK

Art metalwork is the process of making either decorative or useful metal objects by hand. Skilled artists and craftspeople design and make beautiful art metal objects. These may be eating utensils, bowls, trays, pitchers, candlesticks, or trophies. Some of these artists produce jewelry, such as bracelets, rings, brooches, and pins. Many such objects are hammered into shape from metal in sheet form. Platinum, gold, silver, pewter, copper, brass, aluminum, nickel silver, and stainless steel are the art metals used most often.

RAISING

Hammering soft metal reduces its thickness. It causes the metal to stretch. If the same spot is hammered repeatedly with a rounded hammerhead, the metal will bulge. The bulging can change a flat disc of metal into a curved or concave shape such as a spoon, saucer, or bowl. This requires careful hammering and the use of overlapping blows. The process is called **raising.** See Fig. 7-1.

One way to raise metal is by using a block of hardwood, such as maple or birch. The raising block has a shallow depression hammered into the end grain, Fig. 7-1. The metal is shaped against the depression. This works well for shallow objects.

First, cut a disc to the required size and lay out circles about ¼″ (6 mm) apart. Draw circles in pencil with a compass, Fig. 7-2. Do not scratch them in with dividers. Use metal without scratches, since scratches are very dif-

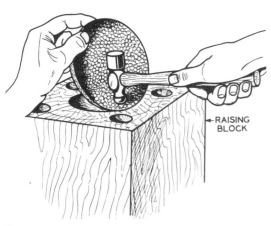

Fig. 7-1.   Raising a bowl.

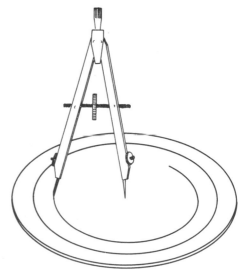

Fig. 7-2.   Use a compass to lay out circles on metal.

ficult to remove. They will not be hammered out in the raising process.

Hold the metal over the raising block. Hammer with a raising hammer or the peen of a ball peen hammer. Begin by hammering **lightly** and evenly on the outside circle. The marks should overlap one another. Striking harder in some places than in others will make the object lopsided. Evenly spaced hammer marks add beauty to the object. If a wrinkle forms at the edge, hammer it out at once, using light blows. After the first circle has been hammered continue by hammering the second circle. Then to each circle until the object has the desired contour.

PEENING AND PLANISHING

Sometimes a hammered finish is desired on art metal objects. Hammered finishes are obtained by **peening** with the peen end of a hammer. The round marks in Fig. 7-3 are made with a hammer which has a ball-shaped peen.

Hammer marks can be applied to both sides of the metal. Fasten one hammer with the peen side up in a vise. Hold the metal on the peen, and strike it with the peen of the second hammer. Interesting finishes may also be made with other types of peen hammers, blunt punches, and chisels.

Planishing means to make smooth. This may be done with a hammer which has a

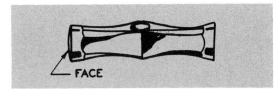

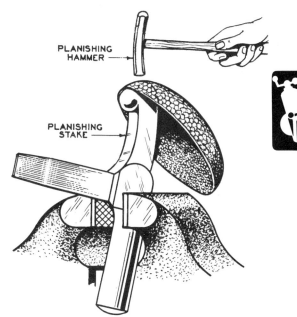

Fig. 7-4.   Hammered finish using a planishing hammer.

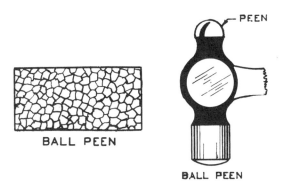

Fig. 7-3.   Hammered finish using a ball peen hammer.

smooth, flat face. It is called a planishing hammer, Fig. 7-4. It levels the uneven surface made by raising the metal, stiffens it, and hardens it. When well done, it makes a beautiful finish. The finely polished surfaces on planishing hammers and stakes should be carefully protected. Nicks and scratches could be transferred to the work and spoil its appearance.

To planish a raised bowl, place it over a planishing stake. Hammer lightly with a planishing hammer. The hammering should proceed in the same manner as for raising. However, the hammer blows should strike the metal at the same point that it touches the stake.

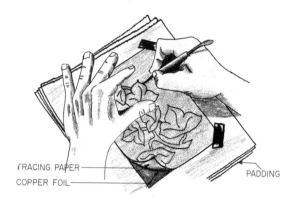

TRACING PAPER
COPPER FOIL   PADDING

Fig. 7-5.   Trace design onto metal foil.

Fig. 7-6.   Traced lines shown on back of foil.

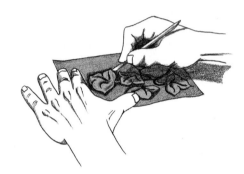

Fig. 7-7.   Press background down.

TOOLING

Metal foil tooling is a process of transferring designs to very thin sheet metal. Certain areas are pressed out from the under side with tools of various shapes and sizes. This procedure adds a three dimensional effect.

Metal foil tooling requires only a few inexpensive tools. The necessary skills are easy to learn. The beginner may feel pleased with the results from the start.

Transferring a Design to Metal Foil

A clearly traced design is essential. It is the basis from which the remainder of the design is tooled. The tracing operation and part of the tooling is done with the metal foil lying on top of a pad. The pad can be made of newspapers, magazines, sheet cork, or felt.

1. Lay the pad on a clean, smooth, work surface.
2. Place the foil on top of the pad with the best side up. This side will be the **front** side of the completed project. The side next to the pad will be referred to as the **back** side.
3. Prepare a traced pattern. Arrange it in the proper position on the metal foil. Secure it with masking tape.
4. Trace over the design with a tracing tool. Hold the thumb and finger on each side of the design being traced to keep it from tearing or slipping. See Fig. 7-5. Use slightly

more pressure on the tool than you would in writing with a pencil. The progress of the tracing may be checked by turning the copper over to show the lines on the back side, Fig. 7-6.
5. Remove the tracing paper.

Tooling a Design on Metal Foil

The property of metals which makes them capable of being drawn out or stretched without breaking is called **ductility**. Some metals are much more ductile than others. Those used for tooled foil projects are not only very ductile, but are also thin. The worker can stretch them in certain areas with hand modeling tools to make them conform to a predetermined design.

1. After the pattern has been transferred to the metal foil, lay the foil on a smooth hard surface. The front side should be up.

Fig. 7-8.   Press out design from back side.

2. Press the background down flat around the traced design. Use the flat side of one of the modeling tools, Fig. 7-7. The background should be flattened frequently during the tooling to keep it from being stretched out of shape.

3. Turn the foil over and lay it on top of the pad. The back side should be up.

4. Use a spoon-shaped, or round modeling tool to press inside the lines forming the design. See Fig. 7-8. Stretch the areas gradually. Check the design often from the front side. The design is pressed out in several steps rather than stretching each part to its total depth. For example, the design may be pressed out about one-fourth of its total depth in the first step. The second step may bring it to about one-half the depth it will have after the tooling is complete. Four or five steps may be necessary to tool some parts of the design to the proper depth.

5. Turn the metal over on a smooth hard surface with the front side up after each tooling step. Flatten the background around the design.

6. Continue tooling. First tool from the back side. Then flatten the background from the front side until the design has been tooled to the proper depth.

7. Keep the details of each part of the design distinct during the tooling steps. Check the design frequently from the front side to see which areas need more tooling. Parts of the design will need little or no tooling from the back side. Sharply defined lines in the design are much more important than heavy tooling.

8. Remember that it is much easier to tool over a design gradually and carefully several times. Too much stretching is hard to correct.

9. Use a wooden tracing tool for very small parts of a design such as stems, small leaves, and veins of larger leaves. The end of this tool may be rounded and polished with fine sandpaper to produce a smooth impression on the copper.

10. Tooling to represent hair, bark on trees, grass, and other details is modeled with the tracing end of a metal tool. An empty ball-point pen can also be used.

11. Tool in the details of the raised design from the front side. Place the finger or heel of the hand in the back side of the design. This keeps the metal from caving in. Modeling clay or putty may also be placed behind the raised design to support it. See Fig. 7-9.

12. To create a stipled effect on the background, see Fig. 7-10.

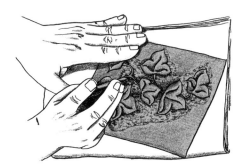

Fig. 7-9.   Use clay to fill background of your design to keep it from being mashed in from front.

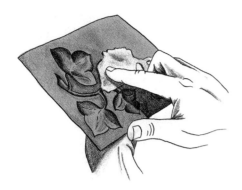

Fig. 7-10. When the design is complete, the background can be tooled to add texture. This is called stippling. Start around the design and work out.

Fig. 7-11. Apply a toning solution.

TONING COPPER WITH LIVER OF SULPHUR

Copper may be decorated by coloring it. The process is called **toning.** You must apply heat or special chemical solutions to the surface. A solution of liver of sulphur (potassium sulphate) and water is used most often. It is easy to prepare and apply.

1. Prepare the solution by breaking off a piece of liver of sulphur about the size of a pencil eraser. Place the small chunk in a small glass of water. Stir it with a wood paddle until dissolved.
2. Check the strength of the solution on a small sample of copper before you apply it to a finished project.
3. Cover the work surface with newspapers.
4. Lay the copper on top of the paper with the front side up.
5. Steel wool the entire front surface. This will remove any material that may hinder the reaction of the solution.
6. The entire piece of copper may be submerged in a large flat tray that holds enough solution to cover the metal. This will give an even color to the surface. The solution may also be applied to the copper with a cloth swab, Fig. 7-11. Use a circular motion. Cover all areas of the design quick-

ly to keep the copper from becoming spotted or streaked.
7. Rinse the copper thoroughly with clear water when the desired color is attained.
8. Polish certain parts of the design with fine steel wool. Study the design carefully to decide which parts should be highlighted. In general, the background is left dark. The remainder of the design is polished to varying degrees of luster.
9. Apply a coat of lacquer over the front surface of the copper to keep it from turning dark due to oxidation.
10. After toning is completed, the background areas are sometimes painted. This furnishes a contrast with the rest of the design. The paint is applied with a small brush.

ETCHING METAL

Most metals can be shaped by **etching** with various acids and other chemical solutions. In the etching process, material is eaten away (decomposed) when exposed to certain solutions. By protecting certain areas of the metal from the acid and leaving others exposed, you can control the etching.

Metal etching is used in the printing industry to produce plates for printing. The elec-

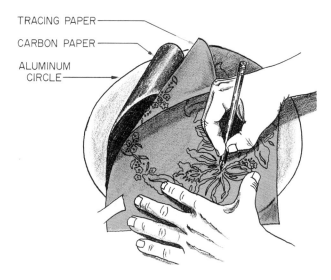

TRACING PAPER

CARBON PAPER

ALUMINUM
    CIRCLE

Fig. 7-12.   The design is transferred to aluminum.

tronics industry also uses the etching process to produce etched circuits on a copper plate. This chapter focuses on the use of etching as an art craft. The same process is involved although the product might be quite different.

Aluminum Etching

and decorative projects. Designs may be transferred to the surface of aluminum. Then certain areas of the design or background are painted with an acid-resisting paint. When the aluminum is placed in an etching solution, the unprotected areas will be dissolved. This leaves

Aluminum projects which are to be etched are first shaped and polished. The design is then transferred to the aluminum. Etching designs are first transferred to tracing paper. The tracing is then placed over carbon paper and copied onto the aluminum, Fig. 7-12.

After you transfer the design to the aluminum, paint the areas to remain shiny with an acid-resisting paint.

1. Paint the design (or background) and back

with acid-resisting paint. Apply the paint with smooth, even strokes. Use only the tip end of the brush, Fig. 7-13.

2. Remove the paint from small lines such as hair or veins of leaves that are to be etched. Let the paint dry for a few minutes so that it

Fig. 7-13.   Paint design with acid-resisting paint.

Fig. 7-14. Scalloping the edge of a tray.

will not flow back into the line. Wipe the paint from each line with the end of the brush handle or a sharpened dowel rod.

3. Let the paint dry according to the directions on the container.

Etching a design into the surface of aluminum is not nearly as hard as preparing the metal and painting the design before etching.

1. Clean the surface to be etched with fine steel wool. This will not affect the surface which is to remain shiny because it is covered with acid-resisting paint.

2. Mix the etching compound according to the directions on the container.

3. Lay the aluminum in an etching pan and pour the solution over it.

4. Leave the aluminum in the solution until the etched portion has reached the desired depth. If a deeply etched design is desired, a new mixture of solution may need to be prepared and the process repeated.

5. Wash the etching solution from the aluminum with water.

6. Remove the acid-resisting paint with mineral spirits, kerosene, or paint thinner.

SCALLOPING

The edges of aluminum trays and other projects may be decorated by a process called **scalloping.** Small circular indentations are made along the edge by tapping a rod-like tool with a ball peen hammer. See Fig. 7-14.

1. Place the aluminum in a vise so that it stands up edgewise. Protect the surface of the aluminum from the vise jaws. Use heavy cardboard or several sheets of paper.

2. Hold the scalloping tool across the top edge of the aluminum.

3. Tap the tool lightly several times with the ball peen hammer to form the impression.

4. Place the scalloping tool in the next position

so that it almost touches the first impression. Tap the tool to form the second impression.

5. Continue around the edge.

FLUTING ALUMINUM DISCS

Trays may be shaped from aluminum discs by bending up the edges at evenly spaced intervals.

1. Make equally spaced marks around the edge of the disc. Cut a paper disc the size of the aluminum and folding it to create 8 or 16 uniformly spaced creases.

2. Make a fluting tool by cutting a notch in a piece of ¼-inch plywood. The length of the notch will determine the depth of the flute.

3. Place the edge of the aluminum disc in the notch at one of the marks.

4. Hold the disc down in the notch as you push it forward to form the first flute, Fig. 7-15.

5. Make the next flute at the mark on the opposite side of the disc.

6. Continue fluting the disc by alternating from one side to the other until it has been fluted at each of the marks.

7. Set the tray on a flat surface to check whether or not the bottom is level. True up or level the tray by pushing down on the opposite sides which are not resting on the flat surface.

ENAMELING

In copper enameling, a specially prepared powdered glass is **fused** to copper surfaces by exposure to very high temperatures. Electric or gas-fired kilns or gas torches may be used. Skills learned in other metalworking activities are used to produce the object to be enameled. This includes sawing, shearing, filing, cleaning, soldering, and polishing.

Enameling of metal is an important industrial process. It is used to apply finishes to various kinds of metal in the production of many items. Refrigerators, kitchen ranges,

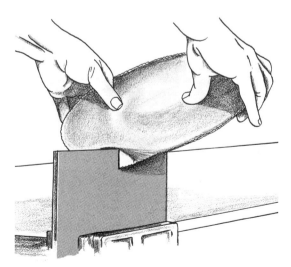

Fig. 7-15.   Fluting a tray.

Porcelain Enamel Institute, Inc.

Fig. 7-16.   Inspecting porcelain enameled mufflers coming from a tunnel kiln.

Fig. 7-17. Clean copper before enameling.

washing machines, and insulation on copper wire used for electronic purposes have enamel finishes. These finishes are durable, attractive, and easy to clean. The heating devices and methods used to apply the enamel in industry are different from those used in the craft shop. The principle of the process, however, is very similar. See Figs. 7-16 and 7-17.

Applying a Base Coat

After the copper base has been shaped and cleaned, apply the first coat of enamel. This will serve as a base coat for any decorations to be added later.

1. Preheat the kiln to about 1500°F (815°C).
2. Apply a light coat of gum solution to surface to be enameled.
3. Lay the copper on a small piece of paper.
4. Select the enamel to be used and place it in a sifting jar.
5. Hold the sifting jar upside down and about 6 inches (150 mm) above the copper.
6. Tap the bottom of the jar with your fingers. This will cause the enamel to sift down on the copper base.

7. Coat the area next to the edges first. Then work toward the center. Adjust the height of the sifting jar so that the copper surface gets a smooth even coating of powder.
8. Continue applying enamel until the copper no longer shows through.
9. Let the gum solution dry.
10. Hold the point of a pencil or similar object against the back side of the copper. This keeps it from sliding as the spatula is shoved under from the front side.
11. Place the copper on an enameling rack, Fig. 7-18.
12. Use an enameling fork to lift the rack carefully into the firing chamber of the kiln.
13. Pour the excess enameling powder back into the container.
14. Leave the project in the kiln until it becomes red-hot. The enamel should have a smooth, slick appearance.
15. Remove the project from the kiln. Place it on an asbestos pad to cool.

A good base coat may require two or three coats of enamel. If you need to apply more, clean the scale from the back and edges of the fired piece. Scrape it with a knife and smooth it with emery cloth or abrasive paper. All the scale must be removed. Even small particles will show up in the enamel as black specks and will not fire out.

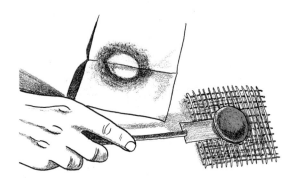

Fig. 7-18. Placing piece on enameling rack.

Sprinkling Powder

Sprinkling is a method of decorating. Enamels of other colors are sprinkled over certain areas of the base coat. Contrasting colors usually look best with the lighter colors applied over a darker base. For example, white enamel sprinkled around the edges of a black base coat gives a very pleasing effect.

1. Apply a base coat of the desired color.
2. Remove the black scale from the back and edges of the copper.
3. Apply the second color over parts of the base coat by sprinkling with the sifting jar. See Fig. 7-19.
4. Place the project in the kiln and let it fire.
5. Pour the excess powder back in the sifting jar.
6. Remove the project from the kiln and let it cool.
7. Remove the black scale from the back and edges of the copper.
8. Polish the exposed surfaces of the copper with steel wool.

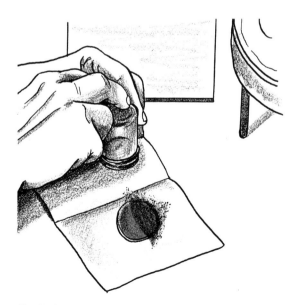

Fig. 7-19. Decorating by sprinkling.

CEMENTING FINDINGS

Metal attachments for cuff links, ear screws, tie clasps, bar pins, and other jewelry are called **findings.** Several kinds of metal cement are suitable for cementing metal findings to the back of enameled jewelry. Some cements come in two separate tubes and must be mixed together before using.

1. Clean the back of the enameled copper and the finding with sandpaper or emery cloth.
2. Mix the cement according to the directions on the containers.
3. Apply a small amount of cement on both the finding and the piece.
4. Stick the two pieces together by applying firm pressure with your fingers.
5. Let the cement dry overnight.

POLISHING EXPOSED COPPER SURFACES

After a project has gone through the firing and soldering operations, the exposed copper must be cleaned and polished. This gives it a finished appearance. The copper undergoes a very fast oxidizing process during the firing. This leaves a black scale on exposed parts.

1. Scrape the black scale from the exposed copper.
2. Polish the copper with a medium grit emery cloth.
3. Rub the sanded surfaces thoroughly with fine steel wool.
4. Polish the surfaces with a cloth saturated with oil and jeweler's rouge to bring a high gloss.
5. Wash the project with hot soapy water to remove the oil and rouge.
6. Dry the project thoroughly. Then apply a coat of metal lacquer over the polished copper, using a small brush. This will prevent the polished copper from developing a dull appearance.
7. If a polished copper finish is not desired, it may be coated with regular enamel.

CASTING

Metal can be heated until it reaches a molten state. It is then poured into molds where it cools and hardens. The mold is then removed, leaving the metal in the same shape as the mold cavity. This method of shaping metal is called **casting.**

Casting is one of the oldest ways of shaping metal. It is still one of the most important processes of our modern metal industry. The production of almost every kind of machine and countless other items requires many metal castings. Our transportation systems are highly dependent upon them. Trains, automobiles, ships, airplanes, and rockets all use hundreds of parts made by casting.

Permanent molds are made from metal. They are used over and over to produce many castings having exactly the same shape. The mold must be made from a material that will withstand the heat of the molten metal poured into it. Nonferrous metals, which have rather low melting points, are generally cast in metal molds.

There are seven main types of casting processes: (1) sand casting, (2) shell-mold casting, (3) die casting, (4) permanent-mold casting, (5) investment casting, (6) plaster-mold casting, and (7) centrifugal casting. Figure 8-1 compares the main features of these casting processes.

PATTERNMAKING

One of the first steps in preparing a sand mold is to make a pattern for the metal casting. Patterns may be made from any material which will hold its shape during molding. Wood is most often used. The people who make these

patterns are highly skilled. They are called **patternmakers.** Simple patterns are made in one or two parts. Some may require several pieces. The sides of the wood pattern are beveled slightly. This makes it easy to lift the pattern from the mold without tearing the sand loose. This bevel is referred to as **draft.**

The molds are made by forming the sand around the pattern. The pattern is then removed to leave a cavity in the sand. The cavity is in the desired shape of the metal casting, Fig. 8-2. After the molten metal is poured and hardens, the sand is removed, leaving the metal casting of the desired shape. Sand molds can be used only one time. To make more castings of the same item, a sand mold must be prepared for each casting.

Making completed castings requires the services of many skilled workers. Engineers design the castings. Drafters make the draw-

Steel Founders' Society of America

Fig. 8-2. When the pattern is removed from the sand, it leaves an accurate cavity into which the molten metal is poured. The core box for the pattern is being constructed behind the pattern.

Fig. 8-1
Comparison of Molds Used to Make Metal
Castings

	Sand Molds			Metal Molds		Special Molds	
	Green Sand Mold	Dry Sand Mold	Shell Mold	Permanent Mold	Die Mold	Investment Mold	Plaster Mold
Chief Materials for Mold	Sand + Clay Binder + Moisture	Sand + Oil Binder + (Oven Bake)	Sand + Resin Binder + (Oven Cure)	Usually Steel	Hardened Steel	Silica Sand + Special Binder + (Air & Oven Cure)	Gypsum + Water
Usual Metals Cast	Most Metals	Most Metals	Most Metals	Aluminum, Brass, Bronze, Some Iron	Alloys of Aluminum, Zinc, Magnesium	Special Alloys	Aluminum Brass Bronze Zinc (Metals that Melt Under 2000° F.)
Surface Finish of Casting	Rough	Rough	Smooth	Smooth	Very Smooth	Very Smooth	Very Smooth
Accuracy of Casting	Not Very Accurate	Not Very Accurate	Fairly Accurate	Fairly Accurate	Very Accurate	Very Accurate	Fairly Accurate
Usual Weight of Castings	Less than 1 Lb. to Several Tons	Less than 1 Lb. to Several Tons	½ Lb. to 30 Lb.	Less than 1 Lb. to 15 Lb.	Less than 1 Lb. to 20 Lb.	Less than 1 Ounce to 5 Lb.	Less than 1 Lb. to 20 Lb.
Cost of Mold	Low	Low	Medium	High	High	High	Medium

ings and blueprints. Patternmakers produce the patterns. Foundrymen pour the molds, and machinists do the finishing work.

SAND CASTING

Sand molds are used for casting any metal. They are well suited for casting iron and steel which have very high melting points. A special sand, called **molding sand,** is used. It contains a portion of clay. It clings together when damp. It remains porous enough to let the steam and gases escape when the molten metal is poured into it. Older types of molding sand (called green sand) are dampened with water. A newer type (such as Petro Bond) uses special oils. Waterless sand is easier to use. It seldom dries out (especially when used with nonferrous metals). It gives smoother castings, but is more expensive. Water is never added. Procedures given here are for green sand. Omit moistening steps if you use waterless sand.

Preparing a Sand Mold

1. Check the sand for the proper moisture content by squeezing a handful into a lump. If the sand clings together, holds its shape and then breaks cleanly, the moisture content is correct. See Fig. 8-3. If the sand falls apart, it is too dry. Sand that sticks to the

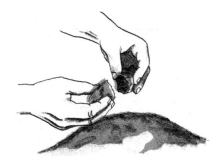

Fig. 8-3.   Molding sand should break cleanly.

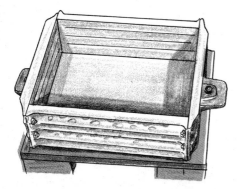

Fig. 8-4.   Drag in position on molding board.

Fig. 8-5.   Ramming the sand.

Fig. 8-6.   Molding board on top of the drag.

hand or leaves excess moisture on the hand is too wet.

2. Prepare the sand for forming the mold. To add moisture, spread the sand out and sprinkle water over it. Then mix it well with a shovel. If the test shows too much moisture, mix in some dry sand.

3. Set the bottom (drag) part of the flask on a molding board with the guide pins down, Fig. 8-4.

4. Arrange the first half of the wood pattern inside the drag on the molding board with the wide, flat surface down. This side of the pattern half has holes in which the dowels of the other half fit loosely.

5. Dust a light coat of parting sand over the pattern and molding board.

6. Riddle the sand (sift it) over the pattern and molding board to a depth of about 2 inches (50 mm).

7. Compress the sand firmly around the pattern with your hands. Ram (tamp) the sand around the edge of the drag with the wedge-shaped end of the rammer, Fig. 8-5. Tamp the other areas with the round end.

8. Shovel around another layer of sand in the drag and repeat the ramming procedure. Continue this process until the drag is full.

9. Strike off the excess sand by raking a board or bar across the top edges of the drag.

10. Place another molding board on top of the drag, Fig. 8-6.

11. Hold the drag and two molding boards together securely and turn them over.

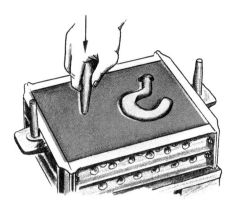

Fig. 8-7.   Placing the sprue pin in position.

Fig. 8-8.   Removing the sprue pin.

12. Remove the top molding board which will reveal the flat side of the pattern.
13. Blow the loose sand from the parting surface, using the bellows.
14. Fit the dowels of the second pattern half in the holes of the first half. The two parts should lie together snugly.
15. Press the small end of the sprue pin into the parting surface to a depth of about ½ inch (12 mm), Fig. 8-7. The sprue pin is used to form the hole through which molten metal is poured into the mold.
16. Sprinkle a thin coating of parting sand over the parting surface and pattern.
17. Fit the cope (top part of flask) in place on top of the drag.
18. Riddle about 2 inches (50 mm) of casting sand over the pattern and parting surface.
19. Form the sand carefully around the pattern and sprue pin with your hands.
20. Fill the remainder of the cope in the same manner as the drag was filled. Work carefully around the sprue pin. Be cautious about hitting it.
21. Loosen the sprue pin by tapping it from the side in every direction. Carefully lift it from the sand, Fig. 8-8.
22. Shape the top of the sprue hole to make a larger opening to let the molten metal flow more easily.

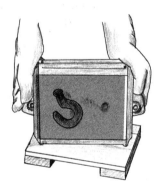

Fig. 8-9.   Set cope on edge.

23. Lift the cope straight up from the drag. Set the cope on edge on top of the mold board, Fig. 8-9.
24. Apply a small amount of water on the sand around the pattern using a small brush or bulb sponge, Fig. 8-10. This operation, called **tempering,** prevents the sand from breaking around the edges of the mold. **Caution:** Too much moisture may cause steam holes in the casting.
25. Cut the gate (channel) from the sprue hole to the mold in either the cope or the drag side of the parting surface. A regular gate

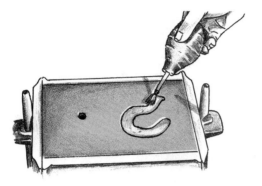

Fig. 8-10. Tempering sand along the pattern.

Fig. 8-12. Lifting pattern from the sand.

Fig. 8-11. Cutting the gate.

Bethlehem Steel Company

Fig. 8-13. Molten iron flowing from industrial cupola.

cutter may be used, or a small piece of tin may be bent in a U shape and used as a cutter, Fig. 8-11. The gate should be shallower where it runs into the mold cavity so that the metal will be thinner in that area and easier to remove from the casting.

26. Secure the point of the draw pin in the wood pattern. Tap the pin sideways all around to loosen the pattern. Lift the pattern straight up from the sand, Fig. 8-12. Both halves of the pattern are removed in this manner.

27. Smooth up the gate. Then blow all the loose sand from the surfaces of the cope and drag, using the bellows.

28. Place the cope back on the drag. The mold is now completed.

Pouring a Sand Mold

Molten metal can be handled safely if you observe safety rules. Wear protective equipment such as a face shield and gloves. Do not let water come in contact with molten metal. One drop may create enough steam to blow out small particles of hot metal. Set the mold on the floor. Stay back as far as possible while pouring the molten metal.

Large furnaces called **cupolas** are used in foundries to melt metal, Fig. 8-13. Some of these can melt several tons of metal at one time. Cupolas usually run constantly for at least several days at a time. The tapping may be done intermittently. Or the metal may flow continuously. The molten metal is drawn (tapped) from the bottom of the cupola. It is carried to the molds by hand or by mechanical means. Most nonferrous metal can be brought to a molten state by heating it in a crucible. Gas or electric furnaces are used.

Metals that have rather low melting points are usually used to pour castings in the industrial arts shop.

Fig. 8-14. Pouring molten metal into the mold.

Fig. 8-15. Mold separated to show the casting.

1. Heat the metal to the proper pouring temperature. This must be somewhat hotter than the melting point of the metal. It must be carried to the mold and poured without cooling and hardening.
2. Heat the ladle to keep the molten metal from cooling and hardening around its sides.
3. Skim off the impurities from the top of the molten metal.
4. Carefully dip the metal from the crucible with the ladle.
5. Hold the ladle close to the mold while pouring to keep the sand from being knocked loose.
6. Pour the molten metal steadily into the sprue hole to keep it filled, Fig. 8-14. This will prevent lightweight impurities from entering the mold or stopping up the sprue hole.
7. Let the casting cool for 15 or 20 minutes. Then break the sand mold away, Fig. 8-15.
8. Remove the sprue from the casting with a hack saw.
9. Finish the casting by filing, grinding, machining, and polishing, as needed.

INDUSTRIAL CASTING PRACTICES

Full Mold Process

The full-mold casting process uses patterns made of polystyrene foam, Fig. 8-16. This material can be shaped very easily. Complex patterns can be made quickly by gluing to-

Fig. 8-16. Polystrene pattern with sprue, gate and runner, and riser system attached.

gether several simple shapes. The sprue, riser (a second hole through which gases and metal can rise), and gate and runner system are also made of polystyrene. They are glued to the pattern. Sand is rammed around the polystyrene pattern in the usual manner, except that the pattern is not removed; hence, the name **full mold.** When the mold is poured, the heat of the metal vaporizes the polystyrene almost instantly. The metal fills the space occupied by polystyrene.

Shell Molding

Another type of sand mold, called a **shell mold,** was developed in Germany in the 1940's. A fine powdered resin is mixed with dry molding sand. The sand-resin mixture is poured onto a metal pattern that is already heated to 400° to 600° F (205° to 315°C). The resin melts and coats the grains of sand. The resin is sticky and causes the grains of sand to stick to each other. At the proper time, the pattern is turned upside down. The excess sand mixture falls off. Only ¼″ to ½″ (6 to 12 mm) of the sand-resin mix sticks to the hot pattern. The pattern is turned upright again. It is then put into an oven to cure (allow the resin to harden). When the sand mold is removed from the oven, it is hard and thin, hence the name **shell mold,** Fig. 8-17.

Die Casting

Casting by forcing melted metal into a die is called **die casting.** See Fig. 8-18. A die is a mold made of metal. It is like a permanent mold

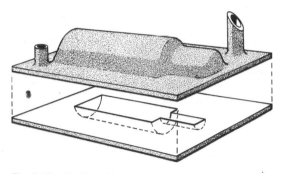

Fig. 8-17.   Shell mold.

Fig. 8-18.   Small die cast parts.

except that the metal is forced into the mold under pressure. The metal is said to be **injected** into the mold. Die-casting machines are made in many sizes. They can cast parts fast. Both the machine and the dies are very expensive. However, many castings can be made from one die.

After the die casting is taken from the mold, it needs very little work to finish it. Often, only trimming the flash and buffing are required. Many die castings are plated with nickel and chrome.

Much hardware is made by die casting. Automobile door handles and hood ornaments, kitchen cabinet handles, and some lamp bases are die castings.

Investment Molds

Most molds are made from a pattern that has positive draft so that it can be withdrawn from the mold. An investment mold is made from a **wax pattern.** This pattern does not have to be tapered because it is melted out of the mold after the mold is made. Therefore, almost any shape of casting can be made from an investment mold. Often, some parts of the wax pattern have straight sides or sides that have negative draft.

Figure 8-19 shows how to make an investment mold. A wax pattern is molded or cut with a warm knife. The pattern is put into a steel flask that looks like a can with its top and bottom removed. A slurry (watery paste of silica and hardener) is poured around the wax pattern. The flask is put on a vibrating table. The vibration packs the slurry against the wax pattern

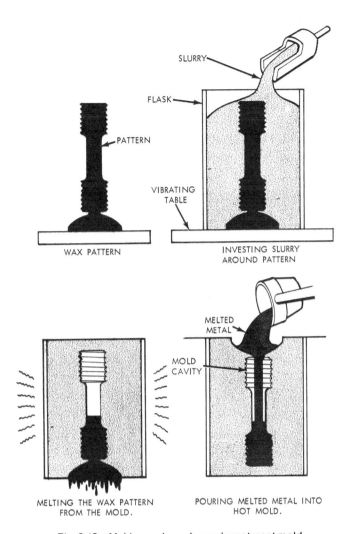

SLURRY

FLASK

PATTERN

VIBRATING
TABLE

WAX PATTERN

INVESTING SLURRY
AROUND PATTERN

MELTED
METAL

MOLD
CAVITY

MELTING THE WAX PATTERN
FROM THE MOLD.

POURING MELTED METAL INTO
HOT MOLD.

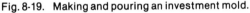

Fig. 8-19. Making and pouring an investment mold.

and removes bubbles of air. Then it is set aside to dry and harden.

Investment mold comes from an old English word, "invest," meaning to enclose or surround. Thus, the wax pattern is invested in a slurry of silica.

Several hours before the mold is to be used, it is turned upside down in a furnace and heated to about 1500° F (815° C). The wax melts and runs out. It leaves the shape of the wax pattern in the mold. Because the wax is melted out of the mold, the mold is sometimes called a **lost-wax mold.** This is called the **lost-wax process.**

The investment mold makes a casting that is very accurate and has a fine smooth surface. The mold is used while still hot from the furnace. It does not chill or cool the melted metal quickly. Therefore, the melted metal can flow into fine cracks and very thin parts of the mold before it becomes solid.

Industry used investment molds to make castings of many sizes and shapes. The dentist casts gold into investment molds to make fillings and other parts for teeth. The jeweler uses investment molds to cast gold, silver, and platinum into rings, bracelets, pins, trophies, and parts for jewelry.

ASSEMBLING

Assembling means putting the parts of something together. For example, many parts are put together to make complete automobiles, Fig. 9-1. Tools for holding, setting, and fastening are needed. This unit describes tools used in assembling. These tools may also be used in other work.

ASSEMBLY TOOLS

Clamps

The **C clamp** is shaped like the letter C. It is made in many sizes and is used to clamp parts together while they are being assembled.

The **parallel clamp** has two steel jaws which are opened or closed by turning two screws. It is used to hold small work. The jaws should always be parallel. This is why the clamp is called a parallel clamp.

Pliers

There are many kinds of pliers, some of which are shown in Fig. 9-2. They are used for holding, gripping, twisting, turning, pulling, and pushing. They also may be used to cut small wire.

The **slip-joint plier,** also known as combination plier, is used for gripping. It can also cut small-size wire. The slip joint makes it possible to grip large parts.

Screwdrivers

Screwdrivers are used to turn or drive screws with slotted heads. They are made in

General Motors Corp.

Fig. 9-1.   Assembling parts for automobiles.

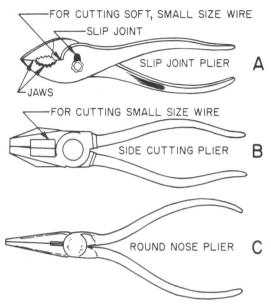

Fig. 9-2.   Pliers.

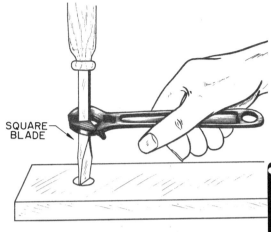

Fig. 9-4.   Turning a screwdriver with a wrench.

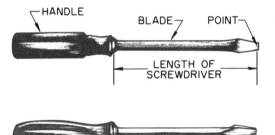

Fig. 9-3.   Parts of a screwdriver.

many sizes and several shapes. The size is measured by the length of the blade. The blade is made of tool steel that is hardened and tempered at the point, Fig. 9-3.

Lay small work on the bench when using a screwdriver. If you hold the work in your hand, you may be injured if the screwdriver slips. Burrs made by a screwdriver slipping out of a screw slot should be filed off to prevent cutting the hands.

The blades on some of the larger screwdrivers are square. A wrench may be used to turn such a screwdriver, Fig. 9-4.

Wrenches

There are many kinds of wrenches, Fig. 9-5. Some are adjustable. This means that they can be made larger or smaller to fit different sizes of bolts and nuts. Others are nonadjustable. That is, they fit only one size bolt or nut. The basic types of wrenches fit these classifications:

Adjustable Wrenches
Monkey wrench
Adjustable-end wrench
Adjustable S-wrench
Vise-grip wrench
Pipe wrench

Nonadjustable Wrenches
Open-end wrench
Box wrench
Socket wrench
Spanner wrench
Hexagonal wrench

Always use a wrench that fits the bolt or nut snugly. When using an adjustable wrench, set the movable jaw until it fits tightly on the

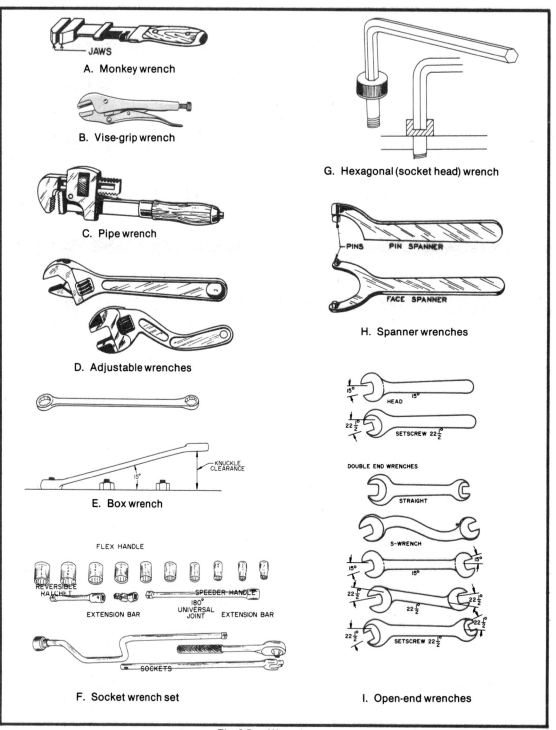

Fig. 9-5.   Wrenches

bolt or nut. Use small wrenches for small bolts and nuts. Use large wrenches on large bolts and nuts.

A wrench is a lever. The longer the handle, the more it multiplies the force of the lever. You can tell by the feel or sense of touch whether a bolt or nut is about to twist off or whether the threads are beginning to **strip.**

MECHANICAL FASTENERS

Rivets are the most common mechanical fasteners used in mild steel work. However, bolts are often used to secure heavy metal where extra strength is needed. Many types of rivets are made to meet various needs. The countersunk-head rivet is used when a flat (flush) surface is desired after the rivet is set. Round-head rivets are used when a flat surface is not required. They are also used when you want the head to show for an ornamental effect.

Fastening with Rivets

1. Select a rivet of the desired diameter and length. Generally, the rivet should be long enough to reach through the metal and extend out the other side about 1½ times its diameter.
2. Drill a hole to fit the diameter of the rivet.
3. Countersink the hole if countersunk rivets are to be set. If both sides of the rivet are to be flush, countersink both sides of the metal.
4. Place the rivet through the holes. Lay the metal on a hard surface with the rivet head down. If the round-head rivet is being set, the head should rest in a rounded depression such as is found on a rivet set tool. Countersunk rivets are placed on a hard, solid, flat surface.
5. Hold the metal and rivet together securely.
6. Set the rivet with a firm blow with the hammer, Fig. 9-6. This causes the rivet to expand and fill the hole.
7. Shape the end of the rivet first with the flat end of the hammer. Then finish the shaping with the peen end, Fig. 9-7. Countersunk rivets may be smoothed out by filing or grinding. See Figs. 9-8 and 9-9.

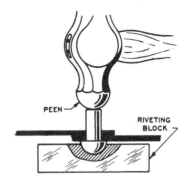

Fig. 9-6.   Strike first in the center of rivet.

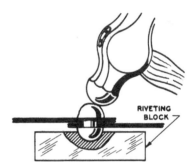

Fig. 9-7.   Rounding the end of the rivet by peening.

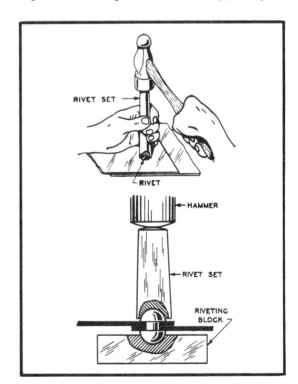

Fig. 9-8.   Forming the rivet head with the rivet set.

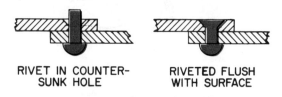

RIVET IN COUNTER-
SUNK HOLE

RIVETED FLUSH
WITH SURFACE

Fig. 9-9. Form rivet head flush with surface in countersunk hole.

Bolts and Screws

Bolts and screws are made in many shapes and sizes. The sizes of bolts and screws are measured by the diameter and length of the body. The head is not included in the length except on flat-head bolts and screws. The kinds most used are shown in Fig. 9-10.

Bolts and screws are used to fasten together parts which have to be separated later. A bolt is used where the worker can get at both sides of the work with wrenches. A screw is used where only one side can be reached with a wrench or screwdriver.

Nuts

There are many different shapes and sizes of nuts. Samples of these are shown in Fig. 9-11. The size of a nut is measured by the diameter of the bolt it fits.

Washers

Washers serve several purposes in fastener assemblies. They are used mostly as a bearing surface for bolts, nuts, and screws. They also serve to distribute the load over a greater area. Washers protect the surface and prevent movement of parts. They are sometimes used with rivets when fastening leather, fiber, canvas, and similar soft materials. The common **flat washer** is a thin, round, metal disk with a hole in the middle, Fig. 9-12.

The size of a washer is measured by the diameter of the bolt that it fits. Flat washers are sold by the pound.

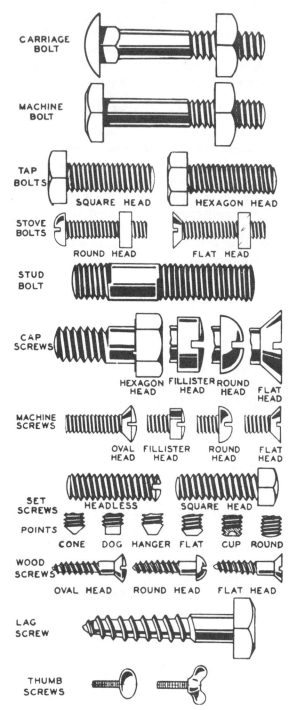

Fig. 9-10. Types of bolts and screws.

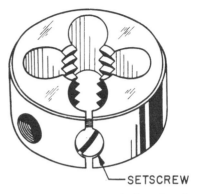

Fig. 9-11. Types of nuts.

Fig. 9-13. Round, adjustable split-threading die.

A. Flat washer

B. Helical spring or lock washer

Fig. 9-12. Washers.

Lock washers serve as a spring takeup between bolts or screws and the workpiece. They also serve to lock the nut or screw in place. This prevents movement or loosening due to vibration. The helical spring lock washer, Fig. 9-12, looks like a coil from a spring.

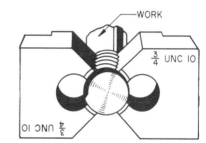

Fig. 9-14. Two-piece threading die.

THREADING WITH TAPS AND DIES

A **threading die** is a round or square block of hardened steel with a hole. The hole contains threads and flutes which form cutting edges. It is used to cut threads on a round bar of metal, such as the threads on a bolt.

One kind of threading die is shown in Fig. 9-13. It is called a round, adjustable, **split die.** It can be set to cut larger or smaller. Another kind is the **two-piece die,** Fig. 9-14. It is made in two halves which match each other. Dies and taps may be bought in a set called a **screw plate.**

THREADING WITH STOCK AND DIE

Cutting threads on a round rod or bolt with a die and stock is called **threading.** The end of the work should be beveled (tapered) to make starting easier. This may be done quickly on a grinder. Hold the work to be threaded upright in the vise. Fasten the die in the diestock. The threads are beveled a little on one side of the die. This makes starting easier and forms the thread gradually. Always start cutting a thread with this beveled side.

Place the die over the end of the work. Grasp the diestock with both hands near the

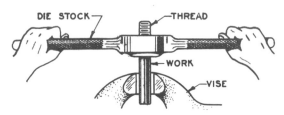

Fig. 9-15. Cutting the thread with the stock and die.

die, press down firmly upon the work and at the same time, slowly screw it on the work **clockwise.** The die cuts the thread as it goes. Be sure that the die goes on squarely. Much skill is needed to do this. After the thread is started, grasp the two diestock handles. With a steady movement, screw the die onto the rod, Fig. 9-15. Since the die actually cuts a groove, the metal chip from the groove must be "broken off." This can be done by backing up the die on every turn. Continuing to cut threads without "backing off" would result in clogging or binding the die. Use oil or some other lubricant to reduce friction.

Cutting Inside Threads with Taps

A **tap** is a screwlike tool that has threads like a bolt and three or four flutes cut across the threads. One end of the tap is square so that it can be turned with a wrench.

Taps are made from carbon steel or high-speed steel. They are hardened and tempered. A set of taps includes a taper tap, a plug tap, and a bottoming tap, Fig. 9-16.

The end of the **taper tap** has about six threads tapered so that the tap will start easily. The threads are cut gradually as the tap is turned into the hole. The taper makes it easier to keep the tap straight.

The **plug tap** has three or four threads tapered at the end. It is used after the taper tap.

The **bottoming tap** has a full thread to the end. It is used to cut a full thread to the bottom of a hole.

Cutting inside threads as in a nut is called **tapping.** After the hole has been drilled with the tap drill, it is ready for tapping — cutting of threads by the tap.

Clamp the work in the vise with the hole in an upright position. First use a taper tap. Clamp its square end in the tap wrench. Grasp the tap wrench with the hand directly over the tap. Place the tap in the hole. Press down and start to screw the tap clockwise into the hole. Use a steady, downward pressure on the wrench to get the thread started.

Skill is needed to keep the tap square with the work. Place a square against the tap to make sure that the tap is square with the work. If it is not square, back it out of the hole a little. Straighten the tap. Use some side pressure to screw it into the hole again.

Continue to turn the tap with one hand until the thread has a good start. Then grasp the tap wrench by the two handles. With a slow, firm, steady movement, continue screwing the tap into the hole, Fig. 9-17. Back up the tap now and then to break and clear away the chips and to make the threads smooth.

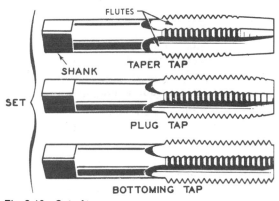

Fig. 9-16. Set of taps.

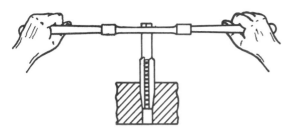

Fig. 9-17. Hold the tap wrench in this manner after thread has been started.

Ordering Metal Fasteners

To be sure of getting the correct metal fasteners, describe them on a bill of materials or order blank as follows:

1. Name of fastener
2. Quantity needed
3. Kind
   a. Kind of material (steel, brass, etc.)
   b. Kind of finish (plain, blued, etc.)
4. Size
   a. Diameter (in inches, millimeters, or gage number) × length
   b. Thread information, if threaded
5. Shape
   a. Shape of head
   b. Shape of point (setscrews only)

Look at suppliers' catalogs for listings of sizes and types of fasteners available.

SOLDERING

Soldering is a process of fastening metals together with a nonferrous metal of low melting point. The metal must adhere to the surfaces being joined. If the solder melts below 800° F (427° C), it is called **soft soldering.** If the solder melts above 800° F (427° C), it is called **hard soldering** or **brazing.** Soldering and brazing are different from welding. In welding, the pieces being joined are melted and fused together. The filler rod for welding is basically the same as the pieces being joined. This is not true of soldering or brazing.

Solder

The best soft solder is an alloy made of lead and tin. For general work, a solder made of one-half lead and one-half tin is used. It is called **50-50 solder** and melts at about 400° F (227° C). The solder must have a lower melting point than the metals to be joined.

Solder comes in bars and in the form of wire on spools. A handy way to buy solder is in the form of hollow wire. Its center is filled with rosin or acid flux.

Special solders are made for soldering aluminum. It takes more heat to melt aluminum solder than solder made of lead and tin.

Paste-type solders are available for use on various metals. Plumbers use them to solder joints and fittings on copper tubing.

Other special kinds of soft solder are available. One is a silver-tin alloy for use on stainless steel. It has a low melting point. It will make solder joints which are up to 10 times stronger than lead-tin solder.

Fluxes for Soldering

Flux keeps the metal surface chemically clean. It stops corrosion, permitting the solder to stick tightly and make a good joint. Fluxes in liquid, crystal, and paste forms are available and can be used for ordinary soldering. Some of these fluxes are for general-purpose use on all common metals. They produce good results.

Soldering a Seam

The surfaces to be soldered must be clean and held together so that heat may be applied. Heat may be applied with electric soldering irons, soldering copper heated in a furnace, or by direct flame from a torch. Hold the soldering iron or copper in one hand and the solder in the other. Tack the seam together. That is, connect the parts in several places with the hot iron or copper and a few drops of solder, Fig. 9-18. This keeps the parts from buckling. Note that a well-tinned copper will hold a drop of solder on the point and make soldering easier.

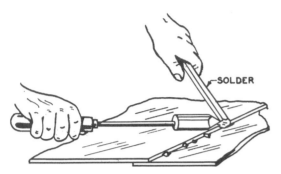

Fig. 9-18. Tacking a seam with drops of solder.

Fig. 9-19. Small AC welder.

Next, hold the hot tinned copper on the edges of the seam and touch the copper with the solder. Move the copper slowly along the seam, a short distance at a time. As the copper melts the solder, put a little along the edge of the seam.

For neat work, remember to use only a little solder. Too much solder on a joint is hard to remove. Also, a thin film of solder makes a stronger joint. The solder must be between the surfaces to be joined, not around them. Then move the soldering iron or copper back to the starting point. Hold one of its flat faces on the seam until the metal gets hot enough to cause the solder that was put along the edge to flow into the seam. Give it time to flow into place before going ahead.

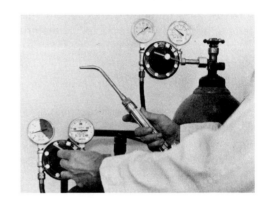

Fig. 9-20. Adjusting acetylene pressure.

Sweat Soldering

In sweat soldering the solder is applied to each piece to be joined. First, clean the surfaces or edges to be joined. Put on a little flux and apply a thin layer of solder. Then press the parts together, using clamps if necessary. Heat until the solder melts and joins the parts together.

When zinc chloride, sal ammoniac, an acid, or any corrosive-type paste flux has been used as a flux for soldering, you must wash the joint in cold, running water. This is done to wash away all traces of the flux. If this is not done, the joint and the metal touched by the flux will turn to a black, dirty color.

WELDING

Welding is a method of attaching two pieces of metal by holding them together, then applying heat until they are in a molten state and flow together. A second metal in the form of a small rod is usually melted and added to the joint as it is welded. This provides added strength.

Two general types of welding are used to fasten metal — electric welding and gas (oxyacetylene) welding. Either type may be used to join soft steel. In electric welding, the metal is heated with an electric arc produced by an electric welding machine. See Fig. 9-19. When the metal reaches a molten state, it flows together. In gas welding, a blowpipe torch which mixes

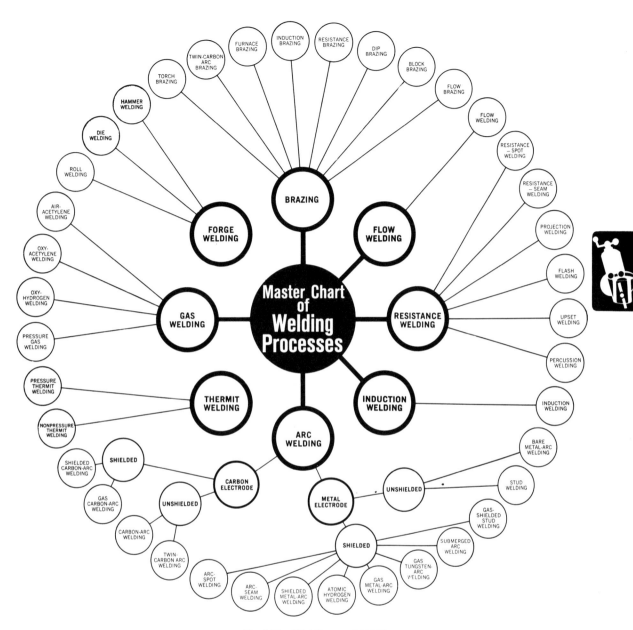

Fig. 9-21. Welding processes.

oxygen and acetylene gas is used to produce a very hot flame. See Fig. 9-20. This heats the metal to a molten state. The many types of welding are shown in Fig. 9-21.

PROPER CLOTHING

The welder must wear protective clothing. This includes the following items:

1. A cloth or leather cap.
2. Goggles or a face shield with colored lenses.
3. Coveralls treated with flame retardant or a full-length apron.
4. Trousers without cuffs and a shirt with full-length sleeves.
5. Leather shoes.
6. Gloves with cuffs that overlap the sleeves.

METAL FINISHING

Metal finishing is the final treatment given to a metal surface. It improves the metal's appearance, makes it wear longer, or keeps it from rusting. Finishing is also done to improve electrical conduction and neutralize the reaction of a metal to certain chemicals. It also improves the value of an object, as when electroplating with precious metals.

This chapter deals mostly with finishes that add decoration to metal objects. Some metal finishes are described in other chapters.

FINISHING MILD STEEL

Outside ornamental ironwork is finished by painting it the desired color. Flatback paint is used for this purpose. Soft steel is often polished to a high sheen. It is then coated with clear lacquer to protect the natural finish of the metal.

Outstanding finishes may be attained by first polishing the metal, then heating it and quenching it in water. Oil is often used in place of water. It is too hazardous, however for the inexperienced worker to use.

Special effects can be given to peened metal. It is first turned dark by heating or painting and then the high surfaces are polished with fine emery cloth. This gives the metal an antique appearance by showing up the peened surface. A coat of clear lacquer should be sprayed or brushed over the peened surface.

BUFFING

Buffing means to polish to a smooth, bright finish. The metal surface is rubbed with a buffing wheel to which a polishing or abrasive compound has been applied. On most metals, this produces a mirror finish. Buffing is also done to smooth a metal surface before electroplating.

Buffing wheels are made of cloth, felt, or leather. Leather and felt make hard wheels. They are used with coarse polishing compounds for the first polishing of rough surfaces. Cloth wheels of cotton muslin are used for intermediate buffing. Soft cotton flannel wheels and fine polishing compounds are used to obtain smooth, bright finishes. Some buffing wheels are set with fiber or wire bristles. They are revolving brushes. Wire brushes are used to deburr, clean, and do some finishing work. A satin finish can be obtained on aluminum by wire brushing. Light scratch brushing may be

Fig. 10-1. Buffing machine.

Fig. 10-2. Washer and nut method of attaching buffing wheel to motor arbor.

Fig. 10-3. Tapered spindle used with jeweler's buffing wheels.

done just before the chemical coloring treatment. It helps obtain uniform coloring.

Buffing machines, also called buffers and buffing heads, look like grinding machines, Fig. 10-1. Some buffing wheels have arbor holes. They are attached to the arbor ends with a washer and nut, Fig. 10-2. Jewelers' buffing wheels have only a pinhole at the center and are screwed directly on a tapered buffing spindle, Fig. 10-3.

Polishing Compounds

Polishing compounds, or buffing compounds, are abrasive materials. They are applied to the buffing wheels to cut and polish the metal. Some of the cutting materials used are lime, tripoli (a powdered limestone), crocus and rouge (two red shades of soft iron oxide), emery and aluminum oxide flour, etc. These are mixed with tallow or some other heavy grease and

Fig. 10-4
Buffing Compounds and Uses

Metal	Compound	
	Roughing	Finishing
Aluminum	Tripoli	Rouge
Brass	Tripoli	Lime
Copper	Tripoli	Lime
Pewter	Tripoli	Rouge
Steel	400 Silicon Carbide	Rouge

The Gorham Company

Fig. 10-5. Buffing.

pressed into bars or cakes. Coarse compounds are used for roughing. Fine compounds are used for final polishing. See Fig. 10-4.

How to Buff

When buffing, always wear safety glasses or face shield. Choose a polishing compound according to the kind of metal to be buffed. Put it on the buffing wheel by holding it against the edge of the revolving wheel. Put only a little polishing compound on the wheel at a time. When the surface of the wheel is coated with the compound, buffing can begin.

The work should be held on the underside of the front of the wheel. If the work is pulled out of the hands, it will then fly away from the operator. See Fig. 10-5. Also, when the work is held on the underside of the wheel, the dust will fly away from the operator. If lots of buffing is to be done, the machine operator should wear a respirator. It filters out the dust and grit created during polishing, Fig. 10-6. The work should be moved and turned as it is held against the wheel. In this way, the wheel rubs every corner and curve of the work. Let the buffing compound do the work of polishing. Pushing the workpiece hard against the wheel only creates friction and makes the workpiece hot. If the polishing is slow, try using a coarser compound first.

When all scratches and blemishes have been removed, change from a wheel with a coarse polishing compound to a wheel with a finer compound. Polish with the fine compound until you are satisfied with the finish. If the work comes from the wheel looking greasy and dirty, too much polishing compound has been put on the wheel. The grease can be removed by

The Gorham Company

Fig. 10-6. The machine operator wears a respirator to keep from inhaling dust.

using a solvent like mineral spirits. Then wash the work with hot water and mild soap or detergent.

SURFACE COATING

Painted, Enameled, and Lacquered Finishes

Paint is often used to decorate and protect metal finishes. It is available in many colors and dries with a flat, or dull, finish. **Flat black paint** is a popular interior finish for wrought iron products. Aluminum paint gives good protection for iron and steel fences, signposts, flagpoles, and other metal products exposed to the weather. A **primer** is a paint which will adhere well to a metal surface and is, therefore, used as a first coat. Some metals require a special primer. Galvanized steel, for example, should be prime-coated with a zinc chromate primer. A good primer for iron and steel surfaces exposed to the weather is red lead.

Safety Note
Leaded primers and paints should never be used indoors. There are many cases of infant poisoning due to chewing objects painted with leaded paints.

Enamel is paint to which varnish or synthetic compounds have been added. It is available in a wide range of colors. It dries hard and is available in a high gloss or semigloss finish. Quick-drying enamels will dry in about four hours. Some enamels are baked onto the metal. Examples are appliances, machines, and tools.

Lacquer dries quickly. It is widely used as a metal finish and is harder and tougher than enamel or paint. Clear lacquer is colorless. It allows the color of the metal to show while protecting it from tarnishing or corrosion. Flat lacquer has no gloss. Most lacquers are made of synthetic materials. They require special solvents for thinning and cleaning. While some lacquers can be applied by brushing, others are made for spraying. Lacquers are also available in many colors.

Lacquer is quite flammable and must be kept away from open flames. Containers should be closed right after use. To protect against noxious and explosive fumes, lacquer should be applied only in a well-ventilated room.

Bronzing is giving an article a metallic bronze color. Powdered brass or bronze is often used for bronzing. If the entire surface is to be a bronze color, the bronze powder may be made into a bronze paint by mixing it with a banana oil. The bronze paint can then be put on with a brush.

If the work is to be only partly bronzed, or spotted, it can first be coated with paint, enamel, or lacquer. While it is still sticky, bronzing powder may be dusted on with a pepper shaker. It may also be blown on with a powder blower, Fig. 10-7. Colored bronzing powders are also available.

Surface Preparation for Painting

Painted, enameled, or lacquered finishes will not stick to the metal unless the metal has been properly cleaned. Scale and rust should be removed from old metal. This can be done by wire brushing, polishing with abrasive cloth, sand blasting, or using chemicals such as "naval jelly." All dirt and dust should be removed by brushing or wiping. This is followed by washing or wiping with a solvent to remove all traces of oil or grease.

For surfaces to be painted or enameled, use mineral spirits as a **solvent**. Use lacquer

Fig. 10-7. Powder blower.

thinner to degrease surfaces to be lacquered. Solvents, such as benzene and carbon tetrachloride, are toxic (hazardous to health) and should be avoided. Gasoline should not be used because it is so highly flammable. Kerosene and diesel fuel leave an oily film to which paint will not adhere.

Surfaces which have been degreased should not be handled with bare hands. Body oil from fingerprints will contaminate the surface. Clean surfaces should have the finishing material applied as soon as possible. The need for cleanliness does not stop when the first coat is applied. Any dust, dirt, or grease that collects between coats must be removed before applying the next coat.

Paint will not adhere to newly galvanized (zinc coated) steel surfaces without **etching.** Etching provides a dull, slightly roughened surface to which the paint will adhere. For etching of galvanized surfaces, use a dilute solution, about 5% hydrochloric, phosphoric, or acetic acid. Wear rubber gloves for protection from the mild acid solution. Wet the surface thoroughly and allow it to dry. Rinse with clear water and allow to dry before painting. Galvanized steel that has weathered to a dull appearance can be painted without etching.

Methods of Applying Paint, Enamel, and Lacquer

Finishes may be applied by dipping, brushing, or spraying. Automated finishing systems in factories use dipping and spraying methods. Custom finishing and touchup is often done with a hand-held spray gun. See Fig. 10-8. Small jobs can be done well with aerosol cans. Excellent finishes can be obtained by hand spraying.

Before spraying a valuable finished piece, practice adjusting and using the spray gun. Also practice thinning the finishing material to proper consistency. If possible, place the surface to be sprayed in a vertical position. The nozzle of the spray gun should be held a constant distance from the surface to be sprayed,

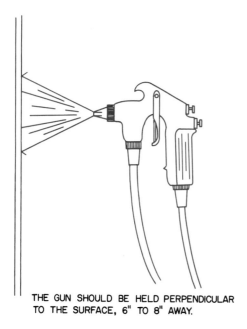

THE GUN SHOULD BE HELD PERPENDICULAR
TO THE SURFACE, 6" TO 8" AWAY.

Fig. 10-8. Paint may be applied by a hand-held spray gun.

about one foot (.3 meter) away. Spraying strokes should run the length of the surface and strokes should overlap each other a little. Wipe away sags and runs immediately. Several thin coats always produce a better finish than one thick coat. This is especially true for spraying.

Brushing is an easy way to finish rather small objects and to use for touch-up. Finishing materials to be brushed on can usually be used directly from the can without thinning. A brush is simpler and quicker to clean than a spray gun. To use a good brushing technique, work the finishing material onto the surface by moving the brush in any direction. Then wipe the excess material from the brush. Lightly stroke the surface to make sure all the brush marks flow in the direction of the longest part of each surface. Enamel dries slower than lacquer. As a result, the lines formed by the brush's bristles get covered as the enamel flows slightly before drying. It is hard to get an even finish by applying lacquer with a brush.

Cleaning Spray Guns and Brushes

Spray guns and brushes should be cleaned right after use. Spray guns should be emptied, wiped, and rinsed with the right solvent. Clean solvent should be sprayed through the gun until all the passages are clean. The gun nozzle is usually taken apart for cleaning. The nozzle of aerosol cans can be kept clean by tipping the can upside down and spraying against scrap paper or cardboard until only clear gas escapes from the nozzle.

Reusable brushes should first be wiped on the edge of the container. Then, as much of the remaining finishing material as possible is removed by brushing on newspaper or paper towels. The brush is then rinsed in a suitable solvent two or three times. It is important to flush out the heel of the brush (where the bristles join the handle). A good way is to hold the solvent-laden brush upside down and squeeze the bristles to aid the flow of the solvent through the heel. After most of the finishing material has been washed out with solvent, the brush is washed with a liquid detergent. Rinse the brush very thoroughly to remove all the detergent. Squeeze as much water as possible from the brush. Reshape the brush and then carefully wrap it in one or two layers of paper towelling to help it hold its shape. See Fig. 10-9. Disposable paintbrushes made of plastic foam are sometimes a good substitute for regular brushes. They also cost less.

Fig. 10-9. Paper towel wrapping helps hold the shape of a clean brush.

HEAT AND CHEMICAL COLORING

Many attractive oxide colors can be obtained on some metals. They are treated with various chemical solutions or simply heated. This treatment causes oxygen to combine with the metal, forming a thin layer of colored metallic oxide. Oxide finishes should always be protected with a coat of lacquer. There are dozens of formulas for chemical coloring solutions. Only a few can be given here.

Copper is easier to color than any other metal. It can be colored yellow, brown, red, blue, purple, or black. The beginner can get good results with the following solution:

> Ammonium sulfide — 1 oz. (29 ml)
> Cold water — 1 gal. (3.7 l)

The work is dipped into this solution. The color produced depends on the length of time the work is left in the solution. When the desired color has been obtained, dry the work in sawdust, clean it, and give it a coat of lacquer.

Ammonium sulfide must be handled with great care because it stains the fingers and has a bad odor. It should be kept in a dark bottle with a glass cover. Ammonium sulfide is only good for coloring copper. It is not good for brass. Potassium sulfide (liver of sulfur) may be used instead of ammonium sulfide.

Brass can be given an antique green finish that will make it look as if it were very old. Make this solution:

> Household ammonia — 4 oz. (118 ml)
> Sal ammoniac — 2 oz. (59 ml)
> Common salt — 2 oz. (59 ml)
> Water — 1 gal. (3.7 l)

Large work can be brushed with the solution. Small work may be dipped into the solution. It may have to be brushed or dipped several times to get the desired color. It should then be rinsed with clear water, dried, and lacquered.

One of the many formulas for chemically coloring steel blue follows:

> Lead nitrate — 1 oz. (29 ml)
> Ferric nitrate — 1/2 oz. (14.5 ml)
> Sodium thiosulfate — 4 oz. (118 ml)
> Water — 1 gal. (3.7 l)

Mix and store the solution in a glass, earthenware, or enameled container. The solution is used hot, 190° to 210° F (88° to 99° C). Soak the clean steel workpiece in the solution until it has the desired color. After careful drying, protect the finish with oil or lacquer.

Oxide colors can be obtained on polished steel by heating to between 380° and 590° F (194° to 310° C). The colors in order of appearance are yellow, brown, purple, violet, blue, and gray. Brighter colors are obtained on highly polished surfaces rather than on dull surfaces. Surfaces freshly polished with abrasive cloth are clean enough for coloring. However, buffed surfaces must be degreased with the right type of solvent.

Since as little as 10° F (-12° C) can cause a change in color, the piece must be uniformly heated if a uniform color is desired. Uniform heating may be done in a furnace.

During heating, inspect the workpiece frequently. As soon as the desired color appears, withdraw it from the heat source. If overheated, the workpiece will have to be cooled, repolished, and reheated. Colored surfaces should be protected with a coat of oil or sealed with a coat of lacquer.

ELECTROCHEMICAL FINISHING

Electroplating, or plating, is the process of coating an object with a thin layer of metal by electrodeposition. Metals that are often deposited by electroplating are copper, nickel, chromium, tin, zinc, brass, gold, and silver. Figure 10-10 shows a typical arrangement for electroplating copper. A direct current is passed from a pure copper plate (anode) to the workpiece (cathode) through a copper sulphate solution (electrolyte). This removes copper from the anode and deposits copper on the cathode. The thickness of the plating depends on how

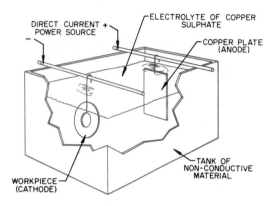

Fig. 10-10. Typical copperplating setup.

strong a current is used and how long the workpiece is left in the plating bath.

Anodizing is an electrochemical finish applied to aluminum and magnesium. Anodizing gives improved corrosion resistance and surface hardness. It is electrically insulating. Some anodized finishes are porous and can be dyed any color. Colored finishes are used on containers such as pitchers and tumblers, sports equipment, appliance trim, hardware, and novelties.

Surface Preparation for Electroplating

Electroplating will exaggerate defects in the surface finish. Therefore, if a smooth, bright plating is desired, surfaces must first be polished to a mirror finish by buffing. This is followed by solvent cleaning. The cleaning removes grease, wax, buffing compound, and other organic contamination. A thin film always remains after solvent degreasing. It is removed by soaking in a hot alkaline cleaner. After a clean water rinse, all traces of oxidation are removed by dipping in an acid solution, also known as **pickling.** After another clean water rinse, the metal should be ready for plating. Parts should not be allowed to dry between steps in the plating cycle. Blisters, pitting, discoloration, peeling, spotting, and skip plating can result from careless and improper cleaning.

SPOT FINISHING

An ornamental finish called **spot finishing** can be produced on flat metal surfaces. To make round, polished spots, cut a short piece of wood dowel of the same diameter as the desired spots. A 3/8″ (10 mm) diameter dowel is often used. Insert the dowel in a drill press chuck. Put oil and abrasive flour on the surface to be spotted. Run the drill press at highest speed and press lightly on the surface. See Fig. 10-11.

Fig. 10-11. Spot finishing.

Chapter **11**   # MACHINE TOOL OPERATIONS

A **machine tool** cuts or shapes metal. The machine holds both the cutting tool and the work piece. The operations of cutting or otherwise removing metal are similar to those discussed in Chapter 4. However, this chapter describes cutting and shaping operations performed by **machine tools.**

There are many kinds of machine tools, but a group of five are referred to as **basic machine tools.** These are lathes, shapers and planers, drill presses, milling machines and grinding machines.

LATHE AND ITS PARTS

Before attempting to operate a lathe you should become familiar with the principal component parts, units, and controls on the lathe. These are named in Fig. 11-1.

The lathe bed is the long part which rests on four legs. The headstock is fastened to the left end of the bed, and the tailstock can be clamped at any point along the bed. The carriage is the part which slides back and forth on the bed between the headstock and the tail-

South Bend Lathe, Inc.

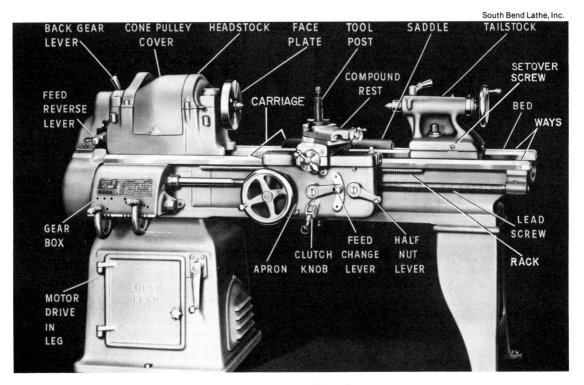

Fig. 11-1.   Lathe and its parts.

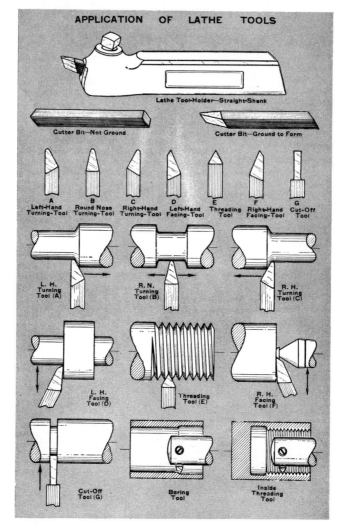

Fig. 11-2. Lathe tool bits and their applications with various lathe operations.

stock. The V-shaped tracks of the bed upon which the carriage and tailstock slide are called ways.

LATHE CUTTING TOOLS

Cutting in the lathe is done with cutting tools, also called lathe tools. The cutting edges are shaped differently depending on the type of toolholder in which they will be mounted, the type of metal to be machined, and the type of cut to be made, Fig. 11-2.

Lathe cutting tools are commonly made of the following materials.

1. High speed steel
2. Cast alloys
3. Cemented tungsten carbide
4. Ceramic

Lathe cutting tools are made into small pieces called tool bits which are held in toolholders. High-speed steel, cast alloy, and carbide-tipped tool bits are small square bars which are held in conventional toolholders. Tungsten carbide and ceramic tool bits are made as throw-away inserts and require special tool holders. Inserts are made in several sizes and shapes.

FACING

Facing is the cutting or **squaring** of the end of a piece of work, Fig. 11-3. Set the cutting tool so that the cutting edge passes through the center and is the only part that touches the work. Then lock the **carriage** to the **bed** by tightening the **carriage lock,** Fig. 11-3. This keeps the tool against the work.

CENTERDRILLING

A piece of metal that is to be **turned** between centers in the lathe must have small, **centerdrilled** holes in both ends. The small holes form **bearing** surfaces so that the work can be held between **lathe centers,** called **centers** for short. (See Fig. 11-5.)

The drilled part of the hole must be deeper than the **countersunk** part to make room for the sharp point of the lathe center. It also holds a small amount of center lubricant to prevent the dead center from overheating. Centerdrilling is done with a combination drill and countersink. The centerdrilled hole must be drilled to the proper depth, as shown at the top on Fig. 11-4. If the hole is either too shallow or too deep, the lathe center will be damaged. Centerdrilling may be done on the drill press or on the lathe.

> ―――― Safety Note ――――
> Before centerdrilling on a lathe, the headstock and tailstock must be in accurate alignment.

The alignment may be checked by aligning the centers. If the centers are not accurately aligned, the point of the centerdrill will break off.

To centerdrill on the lathe, fasten the **centerdrill** in a **drill chuck** which is held in the **tailstock.** Fasten the work in the **lathe chuck.** Then, slide the tailstock so that the centerdrill is near the work, and clamp the tailstock to the **bed.** The centerdrilling is then done by turning the **handwheel** of the tailstock while the work is turning.

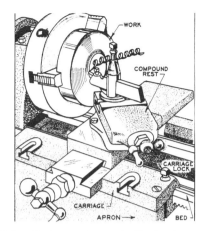

Fig. 11-3. Facing work mounted in chuck.

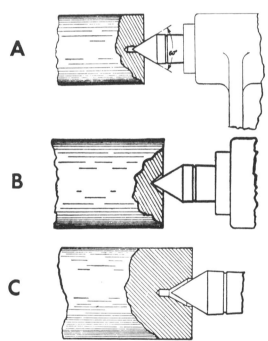

Fig. 11-4. Good and poor center drilled holes.
  A. Good
  B. Hole too shallow and wrong angle.
  C. Hole too deep.

FACEPLATE

The faceplate, Fig. 11-5, is used to drive the lathe dog when turning between centers. Workpieces, or workpiece holding fixtures, are also sometimes bolted directly to the faceplate for machining operations.

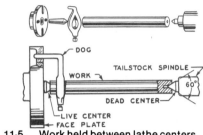

Fig. 11-5.   Work held between lathe centers.

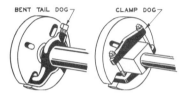

Fig. 11-6.   Fastening lathe dogs to the work.

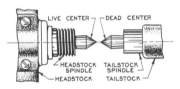

Fig. 11-7.   Proper alignment of lathe centers viewed from above.

LATHE CENTERS

The two lathe centers, called **centers** for short, are used to support the work for turning between centers. (See Fig. 11-5.) The one in the headstock is called the **headstock center** or **live center** because it turns with the **headstock spindle.** The center in the **tailstock spindle** is called the **tailstock center** or **dead center** because it does not turn. Both centers have a Morse taper shank.

The point of the dead center is hardened to make it tough so that when the work rubs on it and causes heat, the point will not wear off. Dead centers are also available with carbide tips for greater wear resistance. Live tailstock centers revolve with the workpiece and thus eliminate the problem of dead center wear and lubrication.

The tailstock center may be removed from the tailstock spindle by turning the handwheel.

This screws the spindle into the tailstock and knocks out the center. To loosen the center in the headstock spindle, put a rod called a knockout rod in the hold at the other end of the spindle. Hold the center with the right hand, and with the left hand tap lightly with the bar.

LATHE DOGS

A lathe dog is used to keep work which is to be turned between centers from slipping. It is clamped on the end of the work, Fig. 11-6, which is then placed between centers. The tail of the dog slips into the slot in the faceplate.

There are many sizes of dogs. Use the smallest one that will slip over the work. The clamp dog is used for large work.

MOUNTING WORK BETWEEN LATHE CENTERS

To place work between centers for straight turning as in Figs. 11-8:
1. Face and centerdrill the work.
2. Screw the faceplate on the headstock spindle.
3. Clamp a **lathe dog** on the work.
4. Be sure the lathe centers are in good condition and the centerdrilled holes in the ends of the work are clean.
5. Put a drop of center lubricant or a mixture of oil and **white lead** in the centerdrilled hole which goes on the tailstock center.
6. Place the work between the lathe centers by sliding the **tailstock** up to the work.
7. Clamp the tailstock to the **bed.**
8. Turning the **handwheel** on the tailstock will set the **dead center** so that the work will move freely on the centers, yet be tight enough to allow no looseness endwise. The **tail** of the dog must fit loosely in the slot of the faceplate.
9. Clamp the **tailstock spindle clamp.**

STRAIGHT TURNING

For straight turning, the work is first placed on **centers,** and the cutting tool is set for cutting. The tool should be set on the left side

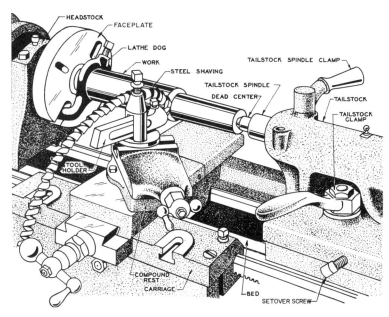

Fig. 11-8.   Straight turning.

on the **compound rest** so that the **lathe dog** will not strike it. For most turning, the compound rest is set at an angle of about 29° or 30° from the crosswise position, as shown in Fig. 11-8. However, when it is necessary to turn very close to the lathe dog or chuck, the compound rest may be set at the crosswise position.

The cutting should be from the tailstock toward the headstock. The reason for this is that when the cutting is toward the headstock, the pressure is on the headstock center which turns with the work. Should the tool feed toward the tailstock, then the pressure is on the dead center. This increases the rubbing, and the point of the dead center may be damaged.

A squeak is a sign that something is wrong. Either the centers are too tight against the work or the dead center needs lubrication.

TAPER TURNING

The machining of tapers is an important operation on the lathe. There are several methods of turning tapers. The one chosen depends on the angle of the taper, the length of the taper, and the number of pieces to be turned. The offset tailstock method is most commonly used. In this method, the right end of the turning will be smaller when the tailstock is moved toward the operator and larger when moved away from the operator. Tapers can also be turned by using a **taper attachment** as in Fig. 11-9.

Tailstock Offset Method

The amount of taper may be specified either by the taper in inches per foot (millimeters per meter) or by the length of the taper and the diameters at the ends of the taper. Two

Fig. 11-9.   Turning a taper with a taper attachment.

formulas will enable you to calculate the tail-stock offset for either specification. These formulas use the following symbols, as illustrated in Fig. 11-10.

T = Total length of stock in inches (mm)
t = Length of portion to be tapered in inches (mm)
D = Large diameter
d = Small diameter
Offset = Setover of tailstock in inches (mm)
tpf = Taper per foot
tpm = Taper per meter

If the taper is given in inches per foot: Divide the total length of the stock in inches by 12 and multiply this quotient by one-half the taper per foot specified. The result is the offset in inches:

$$\text{Offset} = \frac{T}{12} \times 1/2 \text{ tpf}$$

For example, to calculate the amount of tailstock offset for turning work 4" long with a taper of .600" per foot:

$$\text{Offset} = \frac{4}{12} \times 1/2 \text{ .600"}$$

$$= \frac{1}{3} \times .300"$$

$$= .100"$$

Diameters given at ends of taper: Divide the total length of the stock by the length of the portion to be tapered and multiply this quotient by one-half the difference in diameters. The result is the offset in inches:

$$\text{Offset} = \frac{T}{t} \times 1/2 \text{ (D-d)}$$

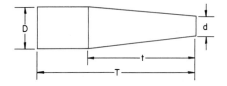

Fig. 11-10. Symbols used in formulas for calculating tapers.

For example, to calculate the amount of tailstock offset for turning work with a length of 6", a tapered length of 3", a large diameter of 1/2" and a small diameter of 1/4":

$$\text{Offset} = \frac{6}{3} \times 1/2 \text{ (.500-.250)}$$

$$= .250"$$

To calculate the tailstock offset using SI metrics, use these formulas:

$$\text{Offset} = \frac{T}{1000} \times 1/2 \text{ tpM}$$

or

$$\text{Offset} = \frac{T}{t} \times 1/2 \text{ (D-d)}$$

An example for the amount of tailstock offset for turning work 100 mm long with a taper of 45 mm per meter:

$$\text{Offset} = \frac{100}{1000} \times 1/2 \text{ 45 mm}$$

$$= \frac{1}{10} \times 22.5 \text{ mm}$$

$$= 2.25 \text{ mm}$$

An example of the amount of tailstock offset for turning work with a 150 mm lenth, a tapered length of 75 mm, a large diameter of 13 mm, and a small diameter of 6 mm:

$$\text{Offset} = \frac{150}{75} \times 1/2 \text{ (13 mm} - 6 \text{ mm)}$$

$$= 7 \text{ mm}$$

To move the tailstock, use the setover screws. The most accurate way to determine the amount of the setover is to measure the offset between the live and dead centers. The cutting edge of the tool must be exactly at the level of the center of the work when cutting tapers.

LATHE CHUCKS

A lathe chuck is used to hold work. It should be screwed on or off the headstock spindle (see Fig. 11-7) while the lathe is stopped. There are three principal kinds of lathe chucks: the four-jaw independent chuck, Fig. 11-11A,

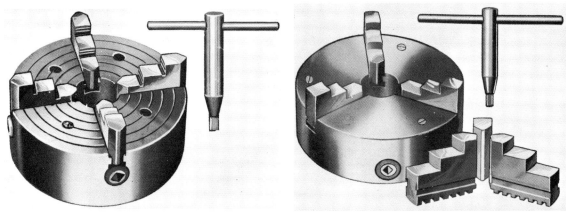

Fig. 11-11. Four-jaw and three-jaw chucks.

the three-jaw universal chuck, Fig. 11-11B, and the collet chucks.

CHUCKING

Chucking means to fasten work in a lathe chuck so that it can be machined.

A four-jaw independent chuck will hold work that is not perfectly round. Each jaw works separately. Place the work in the center of the chuck between the four jaws and tighten them. The circles on the chuck (see Fig. 11-12) help to locate the work in the center. Then run the lathe at a medium speed, rest the hand on the carriage or on the compound rest, and hold a piece of chalk so that it touches only the high spots of the work as it turns, Fig. 11-12. The chalk mark tells which jaws have to be reset. It usually takes a few trials of marking with chalk to get the work to turn without wobbling.

The chalk method of centering work in a four-jaw chuck is accurate enough for many lathe operations. It is satisfactory for jobs which can be completed in one setup. For operations requiring more accurate centering, a dial indicator is used. However, the workpiece should always be centered as close as possible by the chalking method described above, before using the dial indicator.

When centering work in a four-jaw chuck with the use of the dial indicator, it is best to center the work between one pair of jaws at a time. For example, center the work between the jaws numbered 1 and 3, and test with the dial indicator until the same reading is obtained at these locations on the workpiece. When the workpiece has been centered accurately between the first pair of jaws, it can be centered between the second pair easily and rapidly.

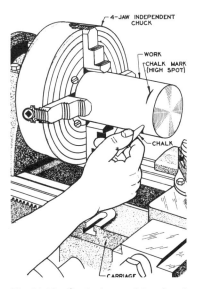

Fig. 11-12. Centering work in a four-jaw chuck.

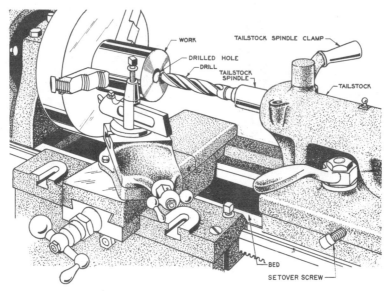

Fig. 11-13. Drilling.

To chuck in a three-jaw universal chuck or a collet chuck, it is only necessary to insert the workpiece and tighten the chuck; the workpiece is centered automatically.

DRILLING, REAMING, AND COUNTERBORING

Drilling, reaming, countersinking, and counterboring — commonly performed with a drill press — can also be performed readily in a lathe. The workpiece is held in a lathe chuck. The drill, reamer, countersink, or counterboring tool is held in the tailstock. The tailstock should always be accurately aligned with the headstock for all hole-machining operations.

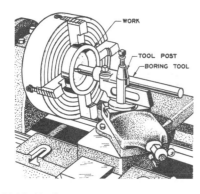

Fig. 11-14. Boring.

For drilling and reaming with small diameter, straight-shank drills; countersinks, and reamers, the tool is held in a drill chuck. The drill chuck is mounted in the tailstock. The tailstock is clamped to the lathe bed so that it does not move. The tool is then fed to the desired depth with the tailstock handwheel.

Larger drills with taper shanks are mounted directly into the tailstock, as shown in Fig. 11-13. Taper-shank reamers, counterbores, and other special taper-shank cutting tools also may be mounted directly in the tailstock for hole-machining operations.

BORING IN A LATHE

It is impossible to make an exact or perfect hole with a drill. A hole may be needed that is larger than an available drill. A hole may be made exactly round (true) by **boring.** There is no limit to the size of a bored hole.

Boring is the cutting and enlarging of a round hole to make:
1. A more exact size.
2. A hole that will not wobble.
3. The hole accurate with its **axis.**

Boring is done with a **boring tool.** There are two kinds of boring tools: the kind that is shown in Fig. 11-14 and smaller **forged** boring tools.

The **tool bit** is held in a **boring bar** which is held in the **tool post** of a lathe, and the cutting is done as shown in Fig. 11-14. The work turns, and the tool is held in a fixed position by the tool post and the carriage moves parallel to the axis of the hole.

CUTTING THREADS ON A LATHE

Screw threads can be cut on work mounted in a lathe, as shown in Fig. 11-15. The workpiece may be mounted in a chuck, or it may be mounted between centers. The threads may be right-hand, left-hand, internal or external threads.

Before cutting screw threads on a lathe, you should be familiar with the kinds of threads, thread fits, classes of threads, and the calculations necessary for cutting threads.

KNURLING

Handles on some tools and screws are made rough in order to give a better grip as the

Fig. 11-15. Cutting thread on a lathe.

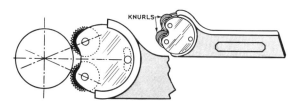

Fig. 11-16. Knurling tool.

handles on scribers. This is called knurling and is done with a **knurling tool** in the lathe, Fig. 11-16. Two small hardened steel wheels or rolls called knurls, turn in the knurling tool when pressed into the rotating work. There are coarse, medium, and fine knurls in diamond and straight line patterns.

THE SHAPER

The shaper, Fig. 11-17, is one of the common basic machine tools. It uses a single-point cutting tool which is very similar to a lathe tool bit. Shapers are used primarily for machining flat surfaces. The flat surfaces may be horizontal or vertical. Grooves, slots, or keyways can be machined with a shaper. Curved surfaces also can be laid out and machined by handfeeding the tool along the layout line.

The workpiece is held tightly in a machine vise or bolted directly to the table. The cutting tool is held in a toolholder which is moved back and forth in a straight line by a ram. The cutting tool peels off a chip each time the ram moves forward on a cutting stroke. The table feed is selected before operating the shaper. The table feeds crosswise during the backstroke of the ram. The machine then makes the next cutting stroke.

Either a shaper or a milling machine may be used for machining flat, vertical, or angular surfaces. Either machine also may be used for machining grooves. Because of a more rapid rate of metal removal, milling machines are rapidly replacing shapers and planers in production machine shops. However, because of the ease of grinding and maintaining shaper tools, the shaper is frequently used in maintenance machine shops, tool and die shops, and school shops.

MILLING MACHINES

A milling machine, Fig. 11-18, is a machine tool which cuts metal with a multiple-tooth cutting tool called a milling cutter, Fig. 11-19. The workpiece is mounted on the milling machine table and is fed against the revolving milling cutter. The speed of the cutting tool and the

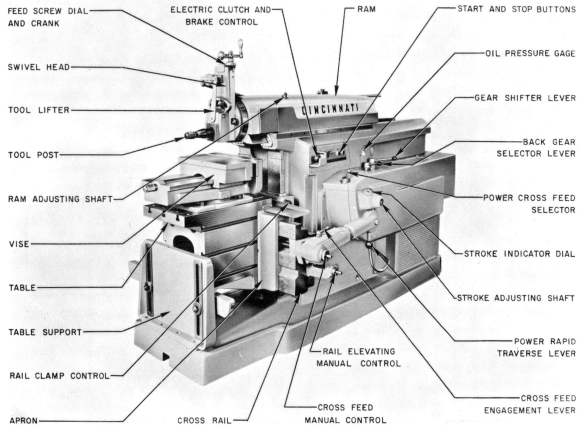

FEED SCREW DIAL AND CRANK

SWIVEL HEAD

TOOL LIFTER

TOOL POST

RAM ADJUSTING SHAFT

VISE

TABLE

TABLE SUPPORT

RAIL CLAMP CONTROL

APRON

ELECTRIC CLUTCH AND BRAKE CONTROL

RAM

START AND STOP BUTTONS

OIL PRESSURE GAGE

GEAR SHIFTER LEVER

BACK GEAR SELECTOR LEVER

POWER CROSS FEED SELECTOR

STROKE INDICATOR DIAL

STROKE ADJUSTING SHAFT

POWER RAPID TRAVERSE LEVER

CROSS FEED ENGAGEMENT LEVER

RAIL ELEVATING MANUAL CONTROL

CROSS FEED MANUAL CONTROL

CROSS RAIL

Fig. 11-17. Plain heavy-duty shaper, showing principal parts.

rate at which the workpiece is fed may be adjusted for the piece being machined.

With heavy-duty milling machines, several kinds of milling cutters may be mounted on the machine arbor for milling several surfaces at the same time. A wide variety of milling cutters is available for use in machining many kinds of surfaces and for performing many kinds of milling operations.

HORIZONTAL MILLING MACHINES

Horizontal milling machines usually have the milling cutter mounted on a horizontal arbor as shown in Fig. 11-19. The arbor fits into the spindle nose which is located on the machined face of the vertical column. The arbor is supported rigidly with an arbor support or overarm support. Milling cutters used on horizontal mill-

ing machine arbors, therefore, have an arbor hole.

End-milling cutters, called end mills can be mounted horizontally in the spindle nose of horizontal milling machines. Thus end-milling operations also can be performed with the cutter operating in a horizontal position on horizontal milling machines. End-milling operations, however, are more commonly performed on vertical milling machines.

VERTICAL MILLING MACHINES

The spindle on vertical milling machines normally is in a vertical position, similar to the spindle on a drill press. However, the head may be swiveled on some machines for angular milling or hole-machining operations shown in Fig. 11-20.

Fig. 11-19. Milling a casting with several cutters mounted on the arbor of a horizontal milling machine.

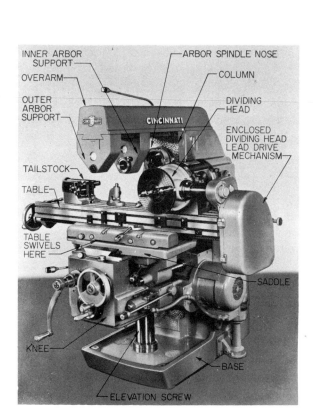

INNER ARBOR SUPPORT — ARBOR SPINDLE NOSE
OVERARM — COLUMN
OUTER ARBOR SUPPORT — DIVIDING HEAD
CINCINNATI
ENCLOSED DIVIDING HEAD LEAD DRIVE MECHANISM
TAILSTOCK
TABLE
TABLE SWIVELS HERE
SADDLE
KNEE
BASE
ELEVATION SCREW

Fig. 11-18. Universal milling machine, showing principal parts.

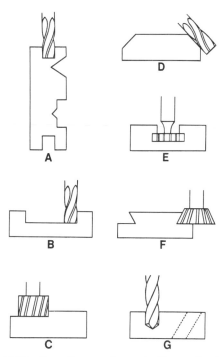

A   D
E
B   F
C   G

Fig. 11-20. Operations performed with a vertical milling machine.
A. Milling a groove.
B. Milling a recessed area.
C. Milling a shoulder.
D. Milling a chamfer.
E. Milling a T-slot.
F. Milling a dovetail.
G. Drilling a hole.

MODERN INDUSTRIAL PROCESSES

Chapter **12**

In earlier chapters, you learned about many cutting, shaping and forming processes. The emphasis was on doing these processes in the school laboratory. Industry uses special machines to do these same processes. These machines are too large and costly to have in the school shop. This chapter describes a few of the industrial processes and machines.

CHEMICAL MILLING

Chemical milling is a process of shaping metal by using strong acid or alkaline solutions. These solutions dissolve away unwanted metal. The process is very simple. It requires neither highly skilled labor nor expensive equipment. It has these advantages:

1. It does not "cold work" the metal as regular machining does.
2. Very large parts can be machined.
3. Any number of the workpiece surfaces can be machined at the same time.
4. Metal can be removed from complex surfaces easily.
5. Since there are no mechanical cutting pressures involved, thin, delicate workpieces such as metal honeycomb can be safely machined.

The procedure for chemical milling begins with the cleaning of the metal. Masking of neoprene rubber or vinyl plastic is then sprayed or flowed on and cured by baking. Areas to be chemically milled are then scribed with the aid of templates. The masking is removed from these areas. The part is then submerged in the chemical milling solution. It remains until the unwanted metal is dissolved away. Rinsing with clean water and removing the masking complete the process.

Chemical milling is most widely used in the aircraft and aerospace industries. Unwanted weight is removed from complex airframe parts without sacrificing strength. **Chemical blanking** is a variation of chemical milling. It produces sheet metal shapes by dissolving all the way through the sheet.

HIGH ENERGY RATE FORMING (HERF) PROCESSES

Explosive forming is a high energy rate forming process which uses the energy released by detonating powerful explosives. The process is used in the aircraft and aerospace industries to make a low number of large sheet

Teledyne Ryan Aeronautical

Fig. 12-1. Explosive formed propellent case for a space vehicle.

metal parts with complex shapes. See Fig. 12-1. High-strength materials which are hard to shape by regular methods are readily made by explosive forming.

There are two types of explosive forming. **Pressure forming** uses the gas pressure produced by slow burning explosives, such as gunpowders. This process must be done in a closed container. **Shock forming** is done in open or partly open containers. The energy from rapidly burning explosives is carried to the workpiece through water, oil, plastic, or other liquid medium. See Fig. 12-2.

Electrohydraulic forming, sometimes called spark forming, is quite similar to shock forming with explosives. Energy rates, however, are lower. The shock waves are created by one or more spark discharges in a liquid medium. The process has most of the advantages of explosive forming.

Electromagnetic forming uses the force of a sudden and intense magnetic field produced by an electric coil being placed inside, around, or next to the workpiece. The workpiece is strongly repelled by the magnetic field. It is forced into the shape of the nonmagnetic die. The process is widely used for the sizing, bulging, and assembling of tubing. Flat pieces can also be formed.

ELECTRON BEAM MACHINING (EBM)

Electron beam machining is done by focusing a high-speed beam of electrons on the workpiece. Sufficient heat is produced to vaporize any known material. Metal removal is very small. The process is used for much the same kind of work as lasers, but it is much more accurate.

The process has disadvantages. Skilled operators are needed and equipment cost is high. There are limits on the workpiece size due to size of the vacuum chamber available. The process also produces X-rays. This requires radiation shielding of the work area.

ELECTRICAL DISCHARGE MACHINING (EDM)

Electrical discharge machining is a process which removes metal by controlled electrical arcing or sparking between tool and workpiece. This occurs while they are submerged in a dielectric (insulating) fluid. See Fig. 12-3. A typical EDM machine is shown in Fig. 12-4. This process is valued for its ability to machine complex shapes in metals of any hardness. It is widely used in making injection and compression molds for rubber and plastic molding, molds for die casting metals, and dies for forging and metal stamping. It is also valuable for its ability to remove broken taps and studs. No tool pressures are involved. This makes EDM useful for machining delicate workpieces, such as metal honeycomb struc-

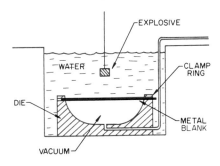

Fig. 12-2. Explosive forming process.

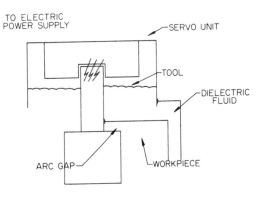

Fig. 12-3. Basic parts of an electrical discharge machining system.

Forging Industry Association

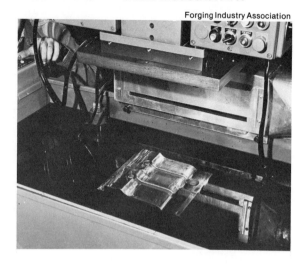

Fig. 12-4. EDM machine with electrolyte surrounding the die block.

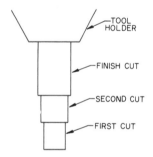

Fig. 12-5. Stepped cutting tool.

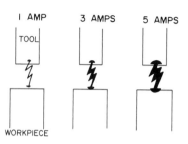

Fig. 12-6. Effect of amperage on the metal removal rate and finish quality.

the amperage settings. Low amperage settings produce slow rates of metal removal and good finishes. High amperage settings produce higher rates of metal removal and poorer finishes. See Fig. 12-6.

Since a gap must exist between the tool and the workpiece, the tool produces a cavity slightly larger than itself. This size difference is referred to as **tool overcut** and is only a very small amount.

To get uniform cutting action and a good finish, a flow of dielectric fluid must be directed through the arc gap to sweep away the chips. The fluid stream may be directed along the tool. Or it may be directed through a hollow tool or through a hole in the workpiece opposite from the point of tool entry.

tures. It has a disadvantage. Only materials that can conduct electricity can be machined.

Electrode (tool) materials include high purity graphite, brass, copper, copper-graphite, tungsten and several tungsten alloys, and zinc alloys. These materials conduct electricity. The EDM process causes much greater tool wear than regular machining processes. Often, several identical tools must be made. One or more is for roughing cuts, and one or more for making finishing cuts. Sometimes stepped tools can obtain the same result as several tools, Fig. 12-5. Metal removal rate depends on

LASER BEAM MACHINING (LBM)

Lasers can machine any known material. The intense heat of the laser beam causes the material to be removed chiefly by vaporization. However, because the rate of metal removal is very small, lasers are only used for jobs requiring a small amount of metal to be removed. Typical jobs include drilling holes, sometimes as small as .001" (0.025 mm), in extremely hard materials such as diamond or carbide for wire drawing dies, and removing minute amounts of metal in balancing parts which spin at high speed.

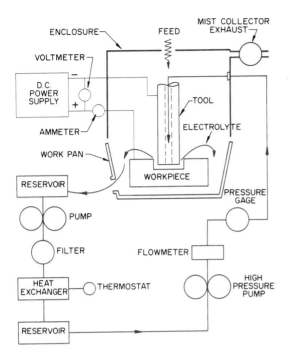

Fig. 12-7. Basic parts of an ECM system.

Since the electrolyte is pumped through the gap between the tool and workpiece at high pressures, the dissolved metal particles are swept away and filtered out. This keeps the particles from being deposited on the tool.

The process is accurate and tool life is very good. This is because (1) the tool never touches the workpiece, (2) it receives no buildup of metal from the workpiece, and (3) it has almost no wear from the flow of electrolyte.

Electrochemical machining can machine any metal that conducts electricity, no matter how hard. With no tool pressure on the workpiece, the process is ideal for machining thin materials and fragile workpieces.

Low metal removal rates as compared to other processes keep ECM from competing with regular machining methods for metals that have good machineability. It excels in machining metals that are difficult to machine, especially when holes or cavities of complex shape must be made. No burrs are produced by ECM. The finishes are bright and smooth and ordinarily do not require polishing.

ELECTROCHEMICAL MACHINING (ECM)

Electrochemical machining is based on the same principles as electroplating. (See Chapter 10.) However, instead of depositing metal on the workpiece, ECM **reverses** the process. The metal is deplated or removed from the workpiece. The basic parts of an ECM system are shown in Fig. 12-7.

In ECM, the tool becomes the cathode and the workpiece the anode. A gap between the tool and workpiece of from .001″ to .010″ (0.2540 to 2.540 mm) is kept to provide space for the flow of electrolyte. The gap also keeps the electrical circuit from becoming shorted. A low-voltage, high-amperage direct current passes from the workpiece to the tool through the electrolyte. This causes metal particles to be dissolved from the workpiece into the electrolyte by electrochemical reaction.

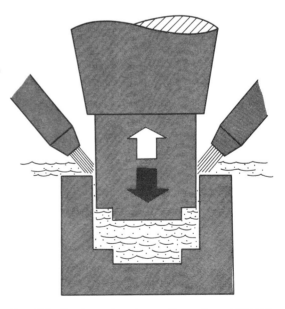

Fig. 12-8. Basic parts of an ultrasonic machining system.

ULTRASONIC MACHINING (USM)

Ultrasonic machining is a process in which fine abrasive particles are suspended in a fluid (usually water). The particles are directed into the gap between the tool and the workpiece, Fig. 12-8. This process is also called **impact grinding.** The tool is vibrated a few thousandths of an inch (millimeters) at an ultrasonic frequency of 20,000 or more cycles per second. This movement causes the abrasive particles to bombard the workpiece with high velocity. This grinds the workpiece to the shape of the tool.

The abrasive particles may be boron carbide, silicon carbide, or aluminum oxide. Grit sizes used range from 280 to 800 mesh. The size used depends on the desired degree of accuracy and the quality of finish desired.

Tools are usually made of soft steel or brass. They must be a mirror image of the shape to be machined. Tool wear is high due to the abrasive cutting action. Cutting involves one or more roughing tools and a finishing tool for each job. The tools are fastened to their toolholders by brazing. A close tolerance is easily held using finer abrasive grits. Finishes are good, being in the vicinity of 20 microinches for ordinary work.

A big advantage of the process is that it can machine materials that cannot conduct electricity. These are materials that cannot be machined by EDM, ECM, or ECG. Glass, ceramic materials, metal oxides, and precious and semi-precious gems are nonconducting materials. They can be machined by ultrasonic machining. This process is also valued because it can machine carbides, tough alloys, and hardened steels. Soft materials, such as carbon, graphite, and plastics are cut as readily as hard materials.

The process is very useful. Any shape can be produced in a workpiece for which a tool can be made.

NUMERICAL CONTROL MACHINING SYSTEMS

Numerical control, abbreviated NC, is a system of controlling a machine or process through the use of a coded number system of information. This information is the input for the machine's control system. See Fig. 12-9. The instructions to the machine are in the form of coded numbers punched into a ribbon of paper tape. The use of the tape may be compared to work done on jigs or fixtures of regular machine tools. The tape can be stored for future use in repeating the same job or process. With some numerical control systems, the coded information is inserted into the control system on punched cards or on magnetic tape instead of punched tape.

Importance of Numerical Control

Automatic operation by numerical control can be used in the operation of many metalworking machines or processes. The use of NC is rapidly increasing for automatic operation of machine tools. Drill presses, milling machines, lathes, boring machines, grinding machines, and punch presses are operated by this process. Numerical control is used for flame-cutting and welding work. Point-to-point NC is used for

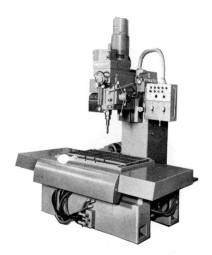

Fig. 12-9. Numerically controlled machining center. This two-axis point-to-point NC machine automatically drills, mills, taps, and bores.

spot welding. Continuous-path NC is used for continuous-path welding.

Numerical control is used with inspection machines. These machines take measurements on parts through the use of sensing probes. They record the difference between the actual size and the specified size. NC is now used for assembly operations such as wiring complex electronic systems. It is also used for tube-forming machines, wire-wrapping machines, and steel-rolling machines.

A more complex system of NC uses various symbols to make automatic drawings with special drafting machines. This kind of NC system generally requires an electronic computer. Abbreviated information from a sketch is fed into a computer. The computer makes many calculations which locate the coordinate points. It provides other required information for drawing lines and curves. When properly equipped, a computer can prepare punched tape. The tape is inserted into the NC system of the automated drafting machine. The NC system reads the tape, commands, and controls the operation of the drafting machine. A drawing is produced automatically.

Basis for NC Measurement

A system of rectangular coordinates is the basis for NC measurements. It is called the **cartesian coordinate system.** See Fig. 12-10. Objects with length, width, and thickness can be described by this rectangular coordinate system. All points of an object are described by imaginary lines perpendicular to the axes. Generally, the horizontal plane includes the X- and Y-axes. In this plane, along the X-axis, all measurements to the right of the origin are in the + X direction. Those to the left are in the − X direction. At exactly 90° to the X-axis, and in the same horizontal plane, is the Y-axis with its plus and minus directions. The Z-axis, with its plus and minus directions, is perpendicular to both the X- and Y-axis.

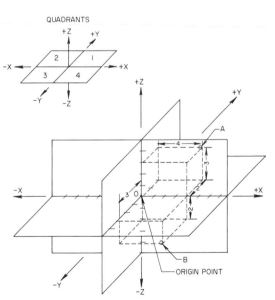

Fig. 12-10. Rectangular coordinate system. All dimensions are given from the point of origin. Point A has coordinates X = + 4, Y = + 2, Z = + 3. Point B has coordinates X = + 4, Y = − 3, Z = − 2.

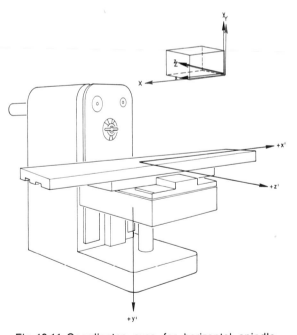

Fig. 12-11. Coordinates axes for horizontal spindle lathes and related machines. Unprimed numbers apply for programmers and operators.

The rectangular system of coordinates describes the dimensions of all parts for numerical-control programming. The axes in this system also are used for machine axis designation. See Fig. 12-11.

In Fig. 12-10, notice that the X- and Y-plane is divided into quadrants. Many NC systems are designed so that all points on an object are located in the first quadrant, as shown in Fig. 12-12. With systems of this type, all positions are designated positive or plus (+). When the object is so located, the positive sign (+) may be omitted when preparing a program manuscript. Study the positions of points A through H until you understand the method for describing points in the first quadrant of the coordinate system.

Machine Axis Designations and Movements

The axes of a machine tool correspond to the main machine movements. The axes are designated in accordance with the axes of the rectangular coordinate system. See Figs. 12-10 and 12-12. Generally, the longest axis of machine travel is designated the X-axis. Notice that the X- and Y-axes are in the horizontal plane in Fig. 12-10 and the Z-axis is in the vertical plane.

An example of a basic machine tool and its axes designations are shown in Fig. 12-11. Pro-

POINT	X	Y	Z
A	5	3	0
B	15	3	0
C	15	7	0
D	5	7	0
E	5	3	4
F	15	3	4
G	15	7	4
H	5	7	4

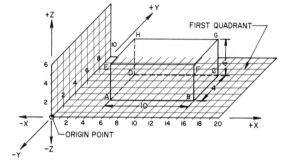

Fig. 12-12. All coordinate points are plus when located in the first quadrant with absolute dimensioning. The + sign may be omitted.

grammers, setup operators, and machine operators need to use only the unprimed numbers or figures such as X, Y, and Z. The primed numbers such as X', Y', and Z' are for the machine manufacturer's use for standardizing the design.

INDEX